Pantry *to* Plate

Pantry *to* Plate

KITCHEN STAPLES
FOR SIMPLE AND EASY
COOKING

EMILY STEPHENSON

CHRONICLE BOOKS
SAN FRANCISCO

Library of Congress Cataloging-in-Publication Data available.

ISBN 978-1-4521-8483-8

Manufactured in China.

MIX
Paper from
responsible sources
FSC™ C008047

Design by **Rachel Harrell**.

Typeset in Sentinel and Brown.

10 9 8 7 6 5 4 3 2 1

Chronicle Books LLC
680 Second Street
San Francisco, California 94107
www.chroniclebooks.com

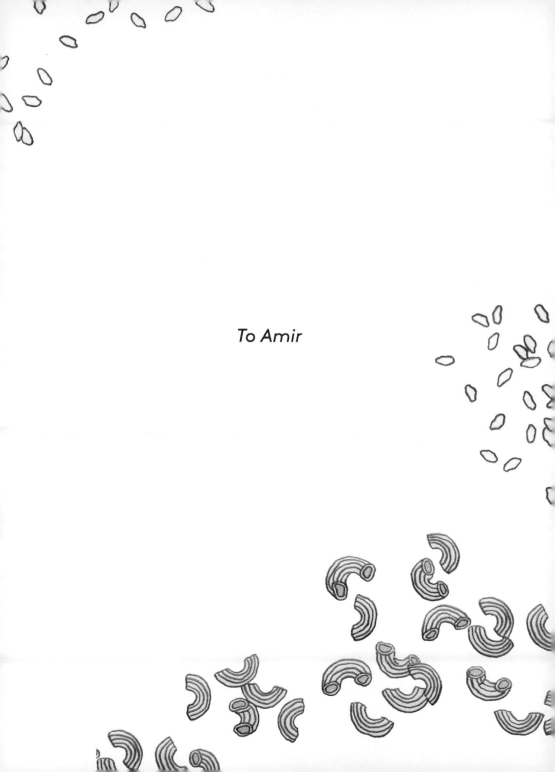

To Amir

TABLE OF CONTENTS

◇◇◇◇◇◇◇◇

INTRO

My favorite part of any cookbook is the pantry section. Whenever I get a new one (which is often), I'll start reading the ingredients section first, ready to get lost in the author's idea of what's delicious, what's important to keep around, and what's absolutely necessary to make a good meal in their mind.

I'll fantasize about living the kind of life where "just whipping something up" for unannounced guests is something I do. Or how much more exciting my no-longer-hurried weeknight dinners will be now that I have a whole part of my fridge dedicated to condiments from around the world, and cabinets full of spices that I will *definitely* use up before they go bad.

I like to imagine what it's like to have the author's cooking life, one that's so organized and seemingly effortless that the cabinets basically fill themselves.

Obviously, they don't.

It's great to get lost in the escapism that some cookbooks can provide, but one way or another, my pantry needs to be stocked; otherwise, I can't *really* cook. I could go to the store every day to buy produce and meat, but I'd still lack the basic ingredients to turn them into a meal. Life's too short to only eat steamed or raw food. And it's definitely too short for unseasoned food.

A full(-ish) cupboard, refrigerator, and freezer is also a gift to all your future selves: the you who works late and gets home ravenous, or is sick and can't leave the house, or is simply tired from all the things that go on in an average day. It means having everything you need to take care of yourself close at hand. It's being ready for the future, even if the future is just two hours from now when you get home from work.

And even if you don't need to be sold on the idea of keeping at least a minimum amount of food in your kitchen, deciding what exactly makes the cut for your personal pantry can be overwhelming. Novice cooks might not know where to begin, and even experienced ones can stock tons of items and still not be able to make a full meal. You might love Mexican food but have a new favorite cookbook that features Mediterranean flavors. Perhaps you grew up eating the same few dishes on rotation. And some ingredients considered essential to a friend might only get used once a year in your home. All of this means endless options for what to buy and cook, and usually after a long day, we want that dinner decision-making process to be as simple as possible.

So, enter this pantry list—fifty cupboard, refrigerator, and freezer ingredients to keep on hand at all times so you can always make a well-balanced meal—and seventy filling, delicious, and healthy recipes you can create using just those ingredients. Think of it as a starting point to a more flexible way to cook that doesn't require much mental energy outside of the kitchen. It means meals you don't have to plan for, cravings you can address ASAP, and a way out of a toast-for-all-meals rut.

The pantry list is not meant to be exhaustive (and yes, it includes salt and pepper, so it truly is *just* fifty). There are some ingredients I love—capers, any vinegar, hot sauce—that didn't make the list. Rather, the finalists are the hardest-working ingredients that can be used in dozens of ways, because the goal of this book is to help you stock your pantry with the minimum amount of food you need to make a wide variety of meals. Expand freely on the list, but make sure you've always got these ingredients at home and you will eat well.

The seventy recipes in this book use only the ingredients from the list, never anything else. I'll note when other fresh produce and herbs (always lots of herbs) would be a welcome addition if you have them, but they're not necessary.

And while hearty, nutritious, and flavorful, these dishes themselves are simple, often streamlined versions of many classics you'll recognize. They will satisfy your hankerings while teaching you the basics of cooking and essential flavor combinations. You'll learn the magic that simple ingredients cooked together can create. For example: Just about everything good starts with onions sautéed in oil.

The recipes aren't meant to be the only food you cook, just as the list of fifty ingredients isn't the only food you should ever have at home. This is your guide for hurried weeknight cooking, relaxed weekend cooking, or for when you've just moved out on your own and are figuring out this whole cooking thing. Because true cooking is making the best of what you've got and getting some-thing delicious on the table—night in and night out.

THE LIST

Here it is: your essentials list, your shopping list, and your (relatively short) path to a good meal.

Note: Some of the recipes require specific types or varieties of the ingredients following (though most are quite flexible), so be sure to check the ingredient lists for any recipes you're planning to make and tailor your shopping list accordingly.

Cupboard

Black peppercorns

Canned black beans

Canned chickpeas

Canned tuna

Preferably in olive oil. Sizes of cans and jars can vary from 3 oz [85 g] to 7 oz [200 g]. I call for 6 oz [170 g] cans in these recipes, but if all you can find is 5 oz [140 g], don't sweat it.

Canned whole tomatoes

With no extra ingredients or flavorings.

Chipotle peppers in adobo sauce

SALT AND HOW TO NOT HAVE TOO MUCH

If you flip through the recipes in this book, you might think I'm joking with these salt amounts. I'm not! All of these recipes were developed with Diamond Crystal kosher salt, the least-salty salt, so 1 tsp of this salt has less punch than the same amount of Morton kosher salt, and a *lot* less punch than sea salt.

If you are using any other salt, cut the amount down to a quarter of what's listed and taste as you go. And remember: Salt preferences are very personal and that's OK! If you're sensitive to salt, hold back, and if you need more, you can always add it later.

Coconut milk

Full fat and not coconut cream!

Cumin

Ground is best, though the whole seeds are great and can be easily ground for the recipes that require it.

Extra-virgin olive oil

I like to believe I'm the type of person who has one for cooking and one for "finishing" but, alas, I always use one reasonably priced bottle for everything.

Garlic

Kosher salt

I use Diamond Crystal, which is the least-salty salt. If you have Morton's or any other variety, *see the sidebar on the facing page for how to convert the amount in recipes.*

Lentils

Brown lentils are the most versatile; green will work for all these recipes too, but might take a little longer to cook.

Long-grain white rice

You can buy plain long-grain rice; I love basmati and jasmine but they might be too fragrant for some uses.

Onions

Yellow or red are fine; I like both for different purposes and will note in the recipes when I have a preference.

Panko bread crumbs

The only bread crumbs worth buying, in my opinion. And I've started to notice them in many more grocery stores, so hopefully they're easy for you to find.

Paprika

Sweet or hot—up to you—just not smoked. It's delicious, but not the right flavor for most of these recipes.

Polenta

I use Bob's Red Mill and recommend you do the same since cooking times between brands can vary greatly. Otherwise, look for fine ground, but not instant, for the recipes in this book.

Potatoes

All-purpose varieties like Yukon gold are best and will work for all recipes.

Red pepper flakes

Rice noodles

Any width you like.

Short pasta

Any cut pasta like macaroni, fusilli, ditalini, etc.

Soy sauce

Spaghetti or linguine

Sweet potatoes

Turmeric

Ground—fresh is great if you can find it, but too specific for this book!

Vegetable oil

Grapeseed or sunflower is my preference, but another neutral vegetable oil works just as well.

Refrigerator

Butter

Since there's no baking in this book, salted and unsalted butter are interchangeable; just dial back any salt you add to a recipe if using the former.

Cabbage

Regular green is best for recipes like Okonomiyaki (page 26), but purple works in a pinch (your Okonomiyaki will be blue but just as delicious).

Carrots

Regular-size carrots please, no babies.

WHAT DOES "1 CARROT" EVEN *MEAN*?

When no vegetable size is listed, then assume that means "medium." And what is medium? When you see a carrot in the store, you don't think, *Holy cow that is a big carrot*, nor do you think, *What a cute little carrot*. You just think, *carrot*. It's a large range, but it really doesn't matter for most of the recipes here. The only time I really specify size is for onions, mostly because unless they're caramelized, I don't want too many in my food.

Celery

Preferably bunches with the leaves, which are more delicious than the ribs (in my opinion).

Eggs

Large, always.

Feta or queso fresco

Both are great and serve the same purpose for this book.

Fresh ginger

Greek yogurt

I prefer full fat!

Kimchi

Cabbage kimchi ideally, but radish kimchi is wonderful and can be chopped for Kimchi Potato Pancakes (page 133).

Lemons

They don't last forever, but they're better off in the refrigerator.

Limes

Ditto.

Miso

White miso and yellow miso are milder than red, and better for these recipes. If you love the taste of red miso, it does work very well in Hearty Miso Soup (page 46).

Olives

Kalamata are the most versatile and great for Greek Chicken (page 170) and Spicy Tuna Pasta (page 97), but whole green varieties will work in all the recipes too (they're especially good in the Chicken Tagine recipe on page 164). Make sure you buy them from an olive bar, as jars are generally overpriced.

Parmesan cheese

Chunks of cheese are a better value than pre-ground, and you can save the rinds to add to soups and stews. Though I wouldn't begrudge you for buying pre-ground, of course.

Tahini

Tofu

Firm tofu will work for all the recipes in this book, but any type can be subbed in. I like silken in Kimchi Tofu Stew (page 126) or Tofu Scramble (page 25), but the difference isn't worth running out to buy a new kind if you already have one on hand. See the sidebar on page 120 for preparing tofu to cook.

Tomato paste

Tubes store longer than cans, but contain less product, so it's up to you which to buy.

Freezer

Bone-in chicken thighs

The additional flavor—especially from the fat in the skin that doubles as your cooking fat— makes the extra cooking time (in comparison to boneless) worth it. If you really must use chicken breasts, know that the cooking times will be longer and you'll need to add cooking oil to the pan.

Broccoli

Greens

I love kale and think it's the most all-purpose option, followed by spinach, then collards, but ideally you can have a mix on hand—and always at least two bags.

Italian sausage

Hot or sweet is fine. In recipes that call for the casings to be removed, just cut a seam down the length of the sausage with scissors and peel back the outside layer (then wash the scissors well).

Peas

Sliced bread

Find a good crusty sourdough variety, and slice it before you freeze it to save a lot of time and potential injury.

Tortillas

Preferably small corn tortillas.

GETTING STARTED AND KEEPING UP

◇◇◇◇◇◇◇◇

Starting a pantry from scratch is daunting. It's a big initial investment to go from empty kitchen to endless possibilities. One of the reasons I find this list so helpful is that it's all the basics in one place. You can easily build on it, but start here.

You may need to get creative to build a pantry since it does require a lot of money up front. If you're not currently flush with cash from graduation gifts, a signing bonus (do those even exist anymore?), or a diligently saved stash, I suggest picking a handful of recipes every week for a few weeks and using your grocery budget to get those ingredients. The pasta you buy in the first week will get used up, but the salt, olive oil, red pepper flakes, and tomato paste will last you for months. After even just three weeks of trying different recipes, you'll have quite a good pantry built up. Then if you do have some additional cash, you can buy extra canned tomatoes, chicken for the freezer, or another loaf of bread.

Say you are able to buy everything on this list in one go. If you have a car, it's not much of an ordeal at all. Simply go to your favorite grocery store, buy at least one, or ideally two, of everything on the list . . . and drive home.

I live in New York City, so I don't have that luxury, and after a decade of

schlepping grocery bags that were probably too heavy, I don't see myself carrying a dozen cans at a time anymore. If you can afford it, I recommend having your initial pantry list delivered by any one of the numerous providers that offer the service (many also offer good deals for first-time customers too). If not, stopping by a grocery store on your way home every night to pick up 20 percent of the list—or, ten ingredients—will mean you're done in one workweek. Not bad at all!

Once you get going, a system to stay on top of the ingredients is a good idea. At some point in my childhood, my dad made a grocery list template with a list of all our pantry staples and kept a stack of them on the refrigerator at all times. We could add things to the list as we finished them. (I don't think we actually kept this up in practice, but maybe you can.) Perhaps today's version is a list template on your phone, though I'm still a sucker for paper shopping lists. You can start with the itemized list in this book and leave empty spaces for produce and other items you can't live without.

Keep track of what you have, and you want to eventually get to a point where you have multiples of an item on hand. Some recipes may require two, or even three, cans of beans or a good amount of tomato paste, and you want to be prepared.

A NOTE ON STORAGE

◇◇◇◇◇◇◇◇

Ingredients need to be close at hand and in a place that makes sense for you to remember you have them and thus use them. Keep a saltcellar and a pepper mill by your workspace within arm's reach of the stove, and everything else visible in your cupboard or refrigerator.

I like to store dry goods in clear glass jars because what I see, I'll use. That can feel like a big investment, but it doesn't have to be. I save any jar after I finish the contents—peanut butter jars are a particular favorite of mine—thoroughly clean the inside, then use baking soda and a lot of elbow grease to scrub the label off the outside. My jar collection is one of my prized possessions and it was (basically) free. I keep a roll of painter's tape and a permanent marker in my kitchen and label each item so I know what I'm working with. It's a handy system I picked up from working in restaurant kitchens that I love to use at home.

Pantry items should be kept out of direct sunlight, preferably out of *any* sunlight. It will cause potatoes to sprout, oil to go rancid (more on that next), and I'm not sure if this is actually true, but I *feel* like it makes lemons and limes go bad faster.

Speaking of food going bad, I had an aha moment when reading an interview with a famous chef in which she talked about olive oil quality and said most Americans cook with rancid olive oil. I had been wondering why my salads never tasted as good as they do at fancy farm-to-table restaurants. I went home, smelled my oil, and immediately knew. The only way I can describe that rancid smell is "waxy."

Once you know what to look out for—whether it be the rice you've had in your cupboard for a few years, that coconut oil you couldn't finish in the (admittedly pretty quick) period before it goes bad, or the spices that are who-even-knows how many years old—you can toss the ingredient whenever it's past its prime. And if you have the opportunity to taste your olive oil before you buy it, or smell rice and beans, you can avoid disappointment from the start. Shopping at stores with a high turnover can also ensure the product you're buying isn't already past its prime.

I don't necessarily think you need to purge your dry goods every 6 months, but when you've reached a year or so on an item and you haven't used it, I'd say it's time to let it go. Canned goods are fine for up to 5 years, and, with the help of this book, shouldn't be sitting around that long anyway.

Related: Your freezer is not a cryogenic chamber. Food will not last forever—it still breaks down, just much more slowly. (I say this not as a judgment, but as someone who had unused specialty flours in the freezer for . . . 6 years.) So label freezer items when you buy them and use them within 6 months.

Lastly, storing leftovers: Unless otherwise noted, you can store any of the recipes in this book in the refrigerator, tightly covered, for up to 4 days.

EQUIPMENT

Nothing extraneous here, just the essential tools used in this book. Restaurant supply stores are a great place to get cheap equipment that lasts for a long time and is sturdy enough to get the job done. Yard sales, moving sales, Craigslist, and Freecycle are also great sources.

Pots & Pans

One large Dutch oven or heavy-bottom pot with a lid

One 10 or 11 in [25 or 28 cm] cast-iron skillet

One large, all-purpose, ovenproof, stainless steel skillet with a lid

One nonstick skillet
Any size is fine, though bigger is always more versatile.

One small (3 to 4 qt [2.8 to 3.8 L]) pot with a lid

Two rimmed baking sheets

One 9 in [23 cm] square baking dish

Utensils

A few wooden spoons

Box grater

Fine-mesh sieve

Fish spatula
The best all-purpose spatula, in my opinion.

Ladle or large metal spoon

Liquid and dry measuring cups
The glass ones for liquids and the stacking type for dry goods; make sure yours are heatproof.

Mandoline
Seems luxurious but you can get one pretty inexpensively, and it's well worth the cost.

Measuring spoons

Metal tongs

Microplane
Perfect for citrus and Parmesan, but you can always use the smallest holes on a box grater.

Pastry brush
Optional but good to have, especially if you like Garlic Bread (page 192).

Silicone spatula

Vegetable peeler

A cheap one is fine since they eventually dull and can't be sharpened.

Whisk

Appliances

Digital scale

Not a big investment, but very useful to have.

Food processor

Great if you can afford one, but things can be chopped by hand until then.

Handheld blender or regular blender

I think you can get by for years with just a handheld (also called an immersion) blender.

Miscellaneous

A few mixing bowls of various sizes

A plethora of kitchen towels

Aluminum foil

Chef's knife

You can get an affordable one at a restaurant supply store; as long as you get it professionally sharpened a few times a year, it will get the job done.

Colander

Make sure it's metal and heatproof.

Long serrated knife

This knife is used mainly for bread. Don't buy an expensive one because they can't be sharpened, so you'd just be throwing away money.

Lots of empty jars and/or clean takeout containers

Painter's tape and a permanent marker

For labeling all of the above.

Paring knife

Pepper mill

Plastic cutting board

Reserved just for raw meat.

Rolling pin

Sometimes, only bashing something will do.

Saltcellar

Or a small bowl to keep salt in—it makes pinching and measuring so much easier.

Wooden cutting board

The biggest that will fit comfortably on your counter.

Eggs for All Meals

This concept of eggs outside of breakfast is, of course, nothing new. But eggs truly are your clutch quick-and-easy pantry ingredient. They are the base for a wide variety of dishes in this chapter that are more exciting and filling than just two hard-boiled eggs (we've all been there). Hopefully, they'll become new favorites in desperate and undesperate times.

"Breakfast" Tacos

This shortcut potato method is both a weeknight lifesaver and a great trick for cooks who also have to do the dishes. It's basically the same method used to make pot stickers—only with a much longer steaming time. If you don't totally trust the method yet, you can use a nonstick pan, but make sure to only use plastic or silicone tools to flip the potatoes.

The rest of the taco components come together easily, then the fun part is assembling them just as you like at the table.

SERVES 4

1 small or ½ large red onion, peeled

2 limes, 1 cut into wedges

12 oz [340 g] waxy or all-purpose potatoes, like Yukon gold

3 Tbsp vegetable oil

1½ tsp kosher salt

½ tsp freshly ground black pepper, plus more for seasoning

½ tsp ground cumin

8 small corn tortillas

1 Tbsp butter

8 large eggs

⅓ cup [40 g] crumbled queso fresco or feta

Cut the onion in half from stem to stem (or halve vertically again if using half a large onion). Chop one half and slice the other half as thinly as you can. Mix the sliced onion with the juice of 1 lime in a small bowl and let the onions pickle while the potatoes cook.

Cut the potatoes into ½ in [12 mm] cubes—more cutting now means less cooking time later! In a large skillet over medium-high heat, mix together the potatoes, chopped onion, vegetable oil, 1 tsp of the salt, the pepper, and the cumin and add ½ cup [120 ml] of water. Over medium-high heat, bring the mixture to a boil, then lower the heat so it simmers steadily. Cover the skillet and cook, swirling the skillet a few times, for 10 minutes. Uncover the skillet and continue cooking, shaking the skillet occasionally, until all the water has cooked off, up to 30 minutes. At this point, stop touching the skillet and let the potatoes cook until they are well browned on the bottom, 4 to 6 minutes. You know the potatoes are done when you can flip them without them sticking and making a mess (you will

cont.

still need a little bit of muscle and a metal spatula)—so resist the urge to touch them too soon.

When the potatoes are ready, turn a gas burner to medium heat, or heat a small skillet over medium heat on an electric stove. Cook the tortillas, one at a time, until they are just barely charred on one side, about 30 seconds. Use tongs to flip each tortilla over and char on the other side, then transfer each one to a plate and cover with a clean towel. Repeat with the remaining tortillas.

Finally, in a nonstick skillet, melt the butter over medium heat. While the butter melts, crack the eggs into a bowl and add the remaining ½ tsp of salt and a few grinds of pepper. Whisk just until no white streaks remain—over-whisking will make the eggs tough. Pour the eggs into the skillet and lower the heat if they bubble rapidly. Cook, stirring slowly but constantly with a spatula so no one section is in contact with the skillet for too long. Continue cooking until the eggs are just a hair undercooked, since they'll continue to cook a bit off the heat, 2 to 3 minutes. Bring the eggs, potatoes, tortillas, pickled onions, and cheese to the table for diners to assemble their own tacos and eat immediately.

FRESHEN IT!
—
Add a handful of fresh cilantro and slice an avocado for garnish. And I know it's not necessarily "fresh," but hot sauce is, obviously, a welcome addition.

Tofu Scramble

I'm including this in the eggs chapter because sometimes the craving for eggs strikes when you're out of eggs, or if you don't eat eggs, or when you're just craving something a little different. Regardless, here's a super-quick, protein-heavy meal that is just as easy, but more exciting, than scrambled eggs. You can use whatever type of tofu you've got on hand—and while I usually go for extra-firm for everything else, silken is great for this recipe since the texture is closer to properly cooked scrambled eggs.

SERVES 4

One 14 oz [400 g] block tofu, any firmness, drained (see page 120)

3 Tbsp vegetable oil

½ onion, any kind, peeled and finely chopped

3 garlic cloves, peeled and sliced

½ tsp kosher salt, plus more for seasoning

2 Tbsp soy sauce

1 tsp ground cumin

1 tsp paprika

½ tsp freshly ground black pepper

½ tsp ground turmeric

FRESHEN IT!
—
Add 2 chopped fresh tomatoes with the onions and/or a few handfuls of fresh spinach with the seasoning mixture.

Break the tofu into bite-size pieces. In a nonstick skillet over medium-high heat, warm the oil until it shimmers. Add the onion, garlic, and salt and cook, stirring often and lowering the heat if the onion starts to burn, until the onion is soft and golden, 8 to 10 minutes. Add the tofu, stir to combine, then spread in an even layer and cook, undisturbed— using all your self-control—until the bottom is browned and crisp, 10 to 12 minutes. Use a silicone spatula to flip sections of the tofu, but it's fine if not every piece is turned over.

In a small bowl, mix together the soy sauce, cumin, paprika, pepper, turmeric, and 3 Tbsp of water. Pour the mixture over the tofu and stir to combine. Continue cooking, stirring once or twice, until the liquid has cooked off, 1 to 2 minutes. Taste and add more salt, if you like. Serve hot.

Okonomiyaki

This is one of my favorite empty refrigerator/on a budget meals—eggs and cabbage, smothered in delicious sauce. Since mayo didn't *technically* make it into the list of fifty ingredients, I included a quick mayo-like sauce that is as savory and tangy as the *Okonomiyaki* sauce-and-mayo combo you'd get in a restaurant. If you have mayo, you can stir in soy sauce to taste, and if you really want to go all out, look for the namesake sauce in a Japanese grocery store.

SERVES 2

"MAYO" SAUCE

4 oz [115 g] silken tofu, drained (see page 120; firm will work too)

½ cup [120 ml] vegetable oil

2 Tbsp soy sauce

1 Tbsp white or yellow miso

1 Tbsp fresh lemon juice

½ tsp kosher salt

BATTER

1 carrot, peeled

6 large eggs, whisked

2 cups [120 g] thinly sliced green cabbage

½ onion, peeled and thinly sliced

1 cup [60 g] panko bread crumbs

1 tsp kosher salt

½ tsp freshly ground black pepper

4 Tbsp [60 ml] vegetable oil

TO MAKE THE SAUCE: Combine all of the ingredients in a blender and purée until smooth. If you don't have a blender, add all of the ingredients except the oil to a food processor and turn on the machine. Slowly drizzle in the oil while the machine is running.

If using firm tofu, you may have to add water, 1 tsp at a time, to get it to a drizzle-able consistency. Transfer the mayo to a zip-top plastic bag. You can make the sauce up to 3 days ahead of time and store it in the refrigerator.

TO MAKE THE BATTER: Use a vegetable peeler to shave the carrot lengthwise into long, thin ribbons. Make as many ribbons as you can before it becomes impossible to keep peeling. Place the shaved carrot in a large bowl with the eggs, cabbage, onion, bread crumbs, salt, and pepper. Fold all the ingredients with a silicone spatula to combine, and keep stirring until all the cabbage is coated in the batter.

In a large skillet over medium-high heat, warm half of the oil until it shimmers. Add half of the vegetable mixture and spread it over the skillet so it makes one large, thin pancake. Cook, lowering the heat if

cont.

the bottom of the pancake begins to burn before the inside is cooked, until the edges brown and you see some bubbles forming in the center of the pancake, 4 to 6 minutes. Run a spatula around the edge to loosen the pancake, then place a large plate or baking sheet over the top of the skillet. Carefully—using towels or oven mitts to protect your hands—hold the plate and skillet together and flip the whole setup over so the skillet is on top and the pancake releases. Slide the pancake back into the skillet, cooked-side up. Continue cooking until the other side is browned and the batter is cooked through, another 3 to 5 minutes. Transfer the pancake to a plate and repeat with the remaining oil and batter.

Cut a small hole from one of the bottom corners of the bag with the mayo and use it to squeeze the sauce in a zigzag or crosshatch pattern on the pancakes. Serve hot.

FRESHEN IT!

Add 4 thinly sliced scallions to the batter along with up to 1 cup [about 130 g] of basically any other vegetable that won't release too much water—think corn kernels, shredded kale, sliced leeks, or bean sprouts.

Shakshuka 101

A simple brunch dish that became trendy for good reason—it's basically what you want to eat for every meal. I call it "101" because after you try the recipe once, you can riff on it in infinite ways: Add a can of chickpeas with the tomatoes, stir in spinach right before baking, or add basically any other vegetable to simmer in the tomato sauce, and you've got a one-dish meal. Highly recommended: plenty of crusty bread on the side.

SERVES 4

3 Tbsp extra-virgin olive oil

1 onion, any kind, peeled, halved, and thinly sliced

3 garlic cloves, peeled and sliced

1 tsp kosher salt, plus more for seasoning

1 tsp paprika, sweet or hot

1 tsp ground cumin

½ tsp freshly ground black pepper, plus more for seasoning

¼ to ½ tsp red pepper flakes, depending on your affinity for heat

One 28 oz [800 g] can whole tomatoes

4 to 8 large eggs (depending on how hungry you are and what else you're serving)

⅓ cup [40 g] crumbled feta or queso fresco

Preheat the oven to 375°F [190°C]. In a large ovenproof skillet over medium-high heat, warm the oil until it shimmers. Add the onion, garlic, and salt. Cook, stirring often and lowering the heat if the onion starts to burn, until the onion is soft and golden, 8 to 10 minutes. Add the paprika, cumin, black pepper, and red pepper flakes and cook, stirring constantly, until fragrant, less than 1 minute.

Pour in the canned tomatoes and their juices and break up the tomatoes with your spoon. Bring the mixture to a boil, then lower the heat so it simmers gently. Cook, uncovered and stirring occasionally, until the sauce has thickened a bit and the tomatoes have started to break down, 15 to 20 minutes. (Now would be the time to add any extras, like one 14 oz [400 g] can of chickpeas, drained, or one 10 oz [280 g] bag of frozen greens.)

cont.

Gently make four (or more) indentations in the top of the sauce. Crack each egg into a small bowl (to prevent eggshells from getting into the dish), and then carefully slide the eggs into the wells in the sauce. Season each egg with a little salt and pepper. Carefully transfer the skillet to the oven and bake until the whites have set and the yolks are still runny, 8 to 10 minutes. Garnish with the feta and serve hot, family style. This dish is best eaten the day it's made.

FRESHEN IT!

Remove the core from 1 red bell pepper and discard, then thinly slice the pepper. Add the pepper to the pan with the onions at the very beginning of cooking.

Egg Curry

The perfect recipe to make a few eggs and a can of tomatoes go very far. It's also a great example of how a few key spices can really make the rest of your pantry sing: Cumin, turmeric, and peppercorns make this curry flavorful without a very long list of ingredients.

SERVES 4

One 28 oz [800 g] can whole tomatoes

3 Tbsp vegetable oil

1 onion, preferably red, peeled and finely chopped

4 garlic cloves, peeled and minced

One 2 in [5 cm] piece fresh ginger, peeled and minced

1½ tsp kosher salt, plus more for seasoning

1½ tsp black peppercorns, crushed

½ tsp ground cumin

½ tsp ground turmeric

4 to 8 large eggs (depending on how hungry you are and what else you're serving)

½ cup [120 ml] coconut milk

Use a blender or food processor to purée the tomatoes and their juices, and reserve. (If you don't have either appliance, squeeze the tomatoes with your hands in a large bowl.)

In a large skillet over medium-high heat, warm the oil until it shimmers. Add the onion, garlic, ginger, and salt. Cook, stirring often and lowering the heat if the onion starts to burn, until the onion is soft and golden, 8 to 10 minutes. Add the peppercorns, cumin, and turmeric and cook until fragrant, less than 1 minute. Pour in the puréed tomatoes and bring to a boil. Lower the heat so the mixture simmers steadily and cook, uncovered and stirring occasionally, until the mixture thickens to a gravy-like consistency, 15 to 20 minutes.

Meanwhile, in a pot large enough to fit all the eggs, bring about 3 in [7.5 cm] of water to a boil. Gently lower the eggs, one at a time, into the water (this helps prevent temperature shock and cracking). Cook the eggs for 8 minutes. While the eggs are cooking, fill a medium bowl with water and ice. When the eggs are done, remove them from the pot and transfer them to the prepared bowl. When the eggs are cool enough to handle, tap each one against a flat work surface and peel, then halve lengthwise. Repeat with the remaining eggs.

Pour the coconut milk into the tomato sauce and stir to combine. Taste the sauce and add more salt, if you like. Place the egg halves into the simmering sauce, cut side down, and spoon the sauce over each egg to warm through. Serve hot. This dish is best eaten the day it's made.

FRESHEN IT!

Substitute 3 large, fresh tomatoes for the canned tomatoes and purée them as in the first step. With the garlic and ginger, add 1 chopped fresh green chile, like a jalapeño or serrano. Cook for the full 20 minutes. For a real treat, add a sprig of fresh curry leaves with the onions, if you can get your hands on some.

Chilaquiles

A brunch staple that's the perfect dinner for people who are too impatient to wait for brunch, like me. Better yet, I took enough shortcuts that this should be ready quickly, for people who are too impatient for dinner on some nights (also like me).

SERVES 4

6 corn tortillas

5 Tbsp [75 ml] vegetable oil

2 tsp kosher salt, plus more for seasoning

One 28 oz [800 g] can whole tomatoes

1 chipotle pepper in adobo sauce, or 1 Tbsp of the sauce if you prefer less spice

½ onion, any kind, peeled and coarsely chopped

2 garlic cloves, peeled

½ tsp freshly ground black pepper, plus more for seasoning

2 limes, 1 cut into wedges

4 to 8 large eggs (depending on how hungry you are and what else you're serving)

⅓ cup [40 g] crumbled queso fresco or feta cheese

Preheat the oven to 375°F [190°C]. Stack the tortillas, then coarsely chop them into chip-size pieces. Put them on a baking sheet and add 3 Tbsp of the oil and 1 tsp of the salt and toss to coat. Spread them into an even layer on the sheet, then transfer them to the oven. Bake until the tortillas are golden around the edges and crisp, 15 to 20 minutes. Keep the oven on and reserve the baked tortillas.

While the tortillas are baking, place the canned tomatoes and their juices, chipotle, onion, garlic, the remaining 1 tsp of salt, and the black pepper into a blender or food processor and blend until smooth. (If you don't have either appliance, chop everything as well as you can and proceed.)

In a large ovenproof skillet over medium-high heat, warm the remaining 2 Tbsp of oil. When the oil shimmers, pour in the sauce and bring to a boil. Lower the heat so the sauce simmers steadily and cook, uncovered and stirring occasionally, until it has thickened and darkened a few shades, and has lost any "raw" flavor, 15 to 20 minutes. Add the juice of 1 lime and taste; add more salt and pepper, if you like.

Fold in the baked tortillas and make sure they are fully coated with sauce. Gently make four (or more) indentations in the top of the sauce. Crack each egg into a small bowl (to prevent eggshells from getting into the dish), and then carefully slide the eggs into the wells in the sauce. Season each egg with a little salt.

Transfer the skillet to the oven and bake until the whites have set and the yolks are still runny, 8 to 10 minutes. Garnish the chilaquiles with the queso fresco and serve hot, with lime wedges on the side.

FRESHEN IT!
—

There are *tons* of fun garnishes you can add to this dish if you have them on hand: 1 fresh jalapeño, thinly sliced; 1 ripe avocado, sliced; ¼ cup [10 g] of chopped cilantro leaves and stems; or 2 to 3 radishes, thinly sliced. Or take some of the onion half left over and finely chop it, then let it sit in cold water while you cook to take some of the bite off. Drain the onion and use as a garnish.

Baked Eggs and Greens

A crazy simple recipe that might be—not so secretly—the most satisfying dish in this whole book. And bonus: It also goes well with just about every kind of starch you can think of—bread, polenta, cooked grains—or as a side to a simple pasta. It's up to you—they'll all be good.

SERVES 4

¼ cup [60 ml] extra-virgin olive oil

1 onion, preferably yellow, peeled and chopped

1½ tsp kosher salt, plus more for seasoning

Two 10 oz [280 g] bags frozen greens, any kind

½ tsp freshly ground black pepper, plus more for seasoning

4 to 8 large eggs (depending on how hungry you are and what else you're serving)

1 cup [240 g] Greek yogurt

½ tsp paprika

1 garlic clove, peeled

1 lemon, cut into wedges

Preheat the oven to 375°F [190°C]. In a large oven-proof skillet over medium-high heat, warm the oil until it shimmers. Add the onion and 1 tsp of the salt. Cook, stirring often and lowering the heat if the onion starts to burn, until the onion is soft and golden, 8 to 10 minutes. Empty the two bags of greens into the skillet—straight from the freezer is fine—and add ½ cup [120 ml] of water and the pepper. Cook, stirring often, until the greens have softened and most of the liquid has cooked off, 2 to 3 minutes (spinach might take 1 to 2 minutes longer).

Gently make four (or more) indentations in the greens. Crack each egg into a small bowl (to prevent eggshells from getting into the dish), and then carefully slide the eggs into the wells. Season each egg with a little salt and pepper. Carefully transfer the skillet to the oven and bake until the whites have set and the yolks are still runny, 8 to 10 minutes.

cont.

Meanwhile, in a small bowl, mix together the yogurt, the remaining ½ tsp of salt, and the paprika. Use a Microplane grater to grate the garlic into the mixture. (If you don't have a grater, reserve the salt and mince the garlic on a cutting board. When the garlic is minced, add the salt and use the side of the blade of your knife to press the salt and garlic into a paste. Add the paste to the yogurt and proceed.)

When the eggs have finished cooking, dollop the yogurt mixture over the greens and eggs in the skillet and serve hot, family style, with the lemon wedges as a garnish.

FRESHEN IT!

Coarsely chop 8 oz [230 g] of white button or cremini mushrooms. Start the skillet over high heat and when the pan is very hot, add the mushrooms and 2 Tbsp of vegetable oil and season with salt. Stir a few times, then cover the skillet and cook until the mushrooms have released all of their juices, 5 to 6 minutes. Uncover the skillet and cook, stirring only once or twice, until the liquid has cooked off and the mushrooms are well browned, 8 to 10 minutes. Transfer the mushrooms to a bowl, wipe out the pan, and proceed with the recipe. Stir the cooked mushrooms into the greens before adding the eggs.

Spanish Tortilla

Eggs and potatoes, Spanish style. The added beauty of this dish is that it's just as good cold as it is at room temperature, and works on its own or as a sandwich filling with some garlicky mayo. Don't be (too) alarmed at the amount of olive oil in the recipe. Much of it gets strained off and you can reuse it for cooking throughout the rest of the week.

SERVES 4

1 lb [455 g] Yukon gold potatoes

½ onion, preferably yellow, peeled

1 cup [240 ml] extra-virgin olive oil

6 large eggs

1½ tsp kosher salt

½ tsp freshly ground black pepper

Peel the potatoes (if you're crunched for time, this step can be skipped) and slice them as thinly as you can manage (if you have a mandoline, this is a great use). Repeat with the onion.

In a large skillet, heat the oil over medium heat. When a potato slice dropped into the skillet bubbles right away, the oil is ready. Add the remaining potato and onion slices. Cook, using a spatula to carefully flip the mixture—without breaking the potatoes—every few minutes, until the vegetables are just barely cooked through, 12 to 15 minutes. You want them to be firm enough that they won't fall apart, but cooked enough that you could eat them as is. Lower the heat if the vegetables start to color at all.

Place a heatproof colander over a large heatproof bowl. Carefully strain the potato mixture into the colander and collect the oil in the bowl. (Let the extra oil cool for a few hours, then store it in a jar in the refrigerator for up to 1 week.) In another large bowl, whisk together the eggs, salt, and pepper, then gently fold in the potatoes.

cont.

Wipe the skillet clean, add 2 Tbsp of the reserved oil, and warm it over medium-low heat. When the oil shimmers, add the egg mixture and use the back of a spatula to flatten the top. Cook the tortilla, lowering the heat if it threatens to burn, until the edges have set, 8 to 10 minutes. Run a spatula around the edges to loosen the tortilla, then place a large plate or baking sheet over the top of the skillet.

Carefully—using towels or oven mitts to protect your hands—hold the plate and skillet together and flip the whole setup over so the skillet is on top and the tortilla releases. Pour another 1 Tbsp of the reserved oil into the skillet, if necessary, and slide the tortilla back in, cooked-side up. Continue cooking until a knife inserted into a few places in the middle comes out clean, another 8 to 12 minutes.

Transfer the tortilla to a cutting board, slice, and serve, or let it cool to room temperature before serving.

FRESHEN IT!

Thinly slice 1 jarred roasted red pepper and serve it on top of the tortilla slices.

Leftovers Frittata

This is a very loose recipe—more of a technique, really—to stretch leftovers or just change things up a bit. It's especially useful for the recipes in the carbs chapter (page 70), as they tend to be a bit generous, servings-wise.

SERVES 2

2 cups [about 115 g] leftover pasta or noodles, or 2 cups [about 240 g] leftover rice, at room temperature

3 or 4 large eggs

¼ cup [60 g] Greek yogurt

¼ to ½ tsp kosher salt (depending on how salty your leftovers are)

Freshly ground black pepper

2 Tbsp extra-virgin olive oil or vegetable oil

FRESHEN IT!
—
Cut the leftovers in half and add an equal amount of chopped fresh vegetables (this also helps leftovers go even further if you want to scale up).

If your food isn't room temperature: Heat an 8 to 9 in [20 to 23 cm] nonstick skillet over medium heat. When the skillet is hot, add the leftovers and cook, stirring occasionally, until they're just warmed through. Remove the leftovers from the skillet and let cool if they're hot enough to potentially scramble the eggs. Wipe the skillet clean.

In a large bowl, whisk together the eggs, yogurt, salt, and pepper, then fold in the warmed leftovers.

In the same skillet over medium heat, warm 1 Tbsp of the oil until it shimmers. Add the frittata mixture and spread into an even layer.

Cook, lowering the heat if it threatens to burn, until the edges have set, 8 to 10 minutes. Run a spatula around the edges to loosen the frittata, then place a large plate or baking sheet over the top of the skillet.

Carefully—using towels or oven mitts to protect your hands—hold the plate and skillet together and flip the whole setup over so the skillet is on top and the frittata releases. Pour the remaining 1 Tbsp of oil into the skillet and slide the frittata back in, cooked-side up. Continue cooking until a knife inserted into a few places in the middle comes out clean, another 6 to 10 minutes. Serve warm or at room temperature.

Soup, *a.k.a.* the Easiest Meal

There are so many reasons to love soup: It's easy to make, it's comforting, it's the perfect packable lunch, and it usually only makes one dirty pan. Consider this chapter my love letter to soup, my go-to pantry meal when the temperature dips below a certain threshold (which isn't *that* low).

Hearty Miso Soup

A truly easy, satisfying, quick meal that you can make as filling as you like—adding chickpeas, frozen peas, broccoli, or a soft-boiled egg to each bowl would not be a bad idea.

SERVES 4

One 1 in [2.5 cm] piece fresh ginger, peeled

2 Tbsp vegetable oil

1 onion, any kind, peeled, halved, and thinly sliced

1 tsp kosher salt, plus more for seasoning

12 oz [340 g] potatoes, any kind, chopped

3 cups [180 g] shredded green cabbage

2 carrots, peeled and chopped

1 tsp crushed black peppercorns, plus more for seasoning

8 oz [230 g] tofu, any firmness, drained (see page 120) and cut into ½ in [12 mm] cubes

½ cup [120 g] white or yellow miso

First, cut the ginger: Stand the ginger on one of the flat cut sides and slice down to make thin planks. When you've sliced the whole piece, stack half of the planks and cut lengthwise into thin matchsticks. Repeat with the other half. Congratulations! You've just made juliennes.

In a large pot over medium heat, warm the oil until it shimmers. Add the ginger, onion, and salt. Cook, stirring often and lowering the heat if the onion starts to burn, until the onion is soft and golden, 8 to 10 minutes. Add the potatoes, cabbage, carrots, and peppercorns and stir a few times to mix.

Pour 6 cups [1.4 L] of water into the pot and bring to a boil. Lower the heat so the soup simmers steadily, add the tofu, and cook, covered, until the vegetables are cooked through and softened, 15 to 20 minutes. In a small bowl, whisk together the miso and ½ cup [120 ml] of water until the miso is completely dissolved.

Turn the heat off and stir the miso mixture into the soup. Taste and add more salt and pepper, if you like. Serve hot. (If you need to reheat the soup, do so over medium-low heat and don't let it boil.)

FRESHEN IT!

—

Add 8 oz [230 g] of sliced shiitake mushrooms with the onions and ginger. You can substitute seasonal produce, like chard, bok choy, or choy sum, for the cabbage in the spring; the kernels from 2 ears of fresh corn for the carrots in the summer; and cubed pumpkin for the potatoes in the fall. The possibilities are endless.

STOCKED

◇◇◇◇◇

You may have noticed that stock is not one of the fifty ingredients. As much as I love to think I'm the type of person who always has homemade stock on hand, that's not the case. I also don't think most store-bought stocks taste very good. So if you're making a quick soup that relies heavily on said stock, you're going to taste it. Quite prominently. Rather, I rely on water and seasonings in the soup to do their thing and find I don't really miss the added flavor.

If you can find a chicken stock you like the taste of, by all means, stock it (pun intended) and use it in any of the recipes that feature chicken already. Commercial vegetable stock, I think, is never worth the money, and beef and fish stocks are too specific to be your go-tos.

Carrot Ginger Soup

Perfect for nights when you want a fast, filling, but not *heavy* dinner, this soup doesn't even require any refrigerated ingredients. It does, however, depend on your ability to purée it, so whether you've got a handheld blender or a standing blender (or a food processor in a pinch), dinner can be yours, quickly.

SERVES 4

3 Tbsp vegetable oil

1 onion, preferably yellow, peeled and chopped

2 garlic cloves, peeled and smashed

One 1 in [2.5 cm] piece fresh ginger, peeled and chopped

1 tsp kosher salt, plus more for seasoning

¼ tsp red pepper flakes

4 cups [560 g] chopped peeled carrots

1 cup [240 ml] coconut milk

1 lime, halved, plus more for seasoning

In a large pot over medium-high heat, warm the oil until it shimmers. Add the onion, garlic, ginger, and salt. Cook, stirring often and lowering the heat if the onion starts to burn, until the onion is soft and golden, 8 to 10 minutes. Add the red pepper flakes and cook, stirring constantly, until fragrant, less than 1 minute.

Add the carrots, coconut milk, and 4 cups [960 ml] of water and bring to a boil. Lower the heat so the soup simmers steadily and cook until the carrots are tender, 10 to 15 minutes. Remove the pot from the heat and squeeze the juice of the lime into the pot. Use a handheld blender to purée the soup directly in the pot; blend for at least 2 minutes to get the soup as smooth as possible.

cont.

If you don't have a handheld blender: Let the soup cool slightly and, very carefully, transfer the soup in batches to a blender or—in a pinch—food processor, and purée until smooth. If using a regular blender, leave a gap between part of the lid and the blender large enough to let steam escape but small enough so that hot soup doesn't splash out and burn you, and never fill the blender more than halfway full. Transfer the puréed soup to a clean pot and repeat with the remaining soup. Bring the puréed soup back to a boil, taste, add more salt or lime juice, if you like, and serve hot.

FRESHEN IT!

Since this recipe is made almost entirely of fresh vegetables anyway (totally possible from your pantry!), you can get creative with the garnishes: cilantro sprigs, chopped scallions or chives, and/or a thinly sliced fresh chile, lke Fresno or serrano.

Sweet Potato and Coconut Soup

This is an all-star pantry cast: You've got coconut milk, you've got canned tomatoes, you've got frozen vegetables, and you've got all the aromatics. So it's no wonder it packs a lot of flavor into one bowl without needing hours to come together. I love it because sweet potatoes are hearty but quick cooking—plus, they add to the delightful rainbow of color.

All you really need to turn this into a meal is some flatbread, or you could reduce the liquid a bit and treat it more like a stew—eaten over Plain White Rice (page 72). Whatever you do, don't forget the lime wedges.

SERVES 4

3 Tbsp vegetable oil

1 onion, any kind, peeled and chopped

3 garlic cloves, peeled

One 1 in [2.5 cm] piece fresh ginger, peeled and chopped

1 tsp kosher salt, plus more for seasoning

1 cup [240 g] canned tomatoes, drained and chopped

½ tsp ground turmeric

½ tsp red pepper flakes

1 lb [455 g] sweet potatoes, cut into ½ in [12 mm] cubes

One 14 oz [420 ml] can coconut milk

cont.

In a large pot over medium-high heat, warm the oil until it shimmers. Add the onion, garlic, ginger, and salt to the pot. Cook, stirring often and lowering the heat if the onion starts to burn, until the onion is soft and golden, 8 to 10 minutes. Add the tomatoes and cook, continuing to stir often, until the pan is dry and the tomatoes are slightly browned in spots, 3 to 5 minutes. Add the turmeric and red pepper flakes and cook until fragrant, less than 1 minute.

Stir in the sweet potatoes, then pour in the coconut milk and 3 cups [720 ml] of water. Bring the mixture to a boil, then lower the heat so it simmers steadily. Cook, covered, until the sweet potatoes are just barely

cont.

One 10 oz [280 g] package frozen greens

1 cup [120 g] frozen peas

Lime wedges, for serving

tender, 10 to 12 minutes. Add the greens and peas and cook until they are warmed through and the sweet potatoes are fully tender, another 5 to 6 minutes. Taste and add more salt, if necessary. Serve hot, with the lime wedges as garnish.

FRESHEN IT!

To change things up sometimes, I like to make an aromatic, sofrito-esque paste: Place the onion, ginger, and garlic in a blender along with the stems of half a bunch of cilantro and 1 seeded jalapeño. Add a splash of water and a big pinch of salt, then purée until smooth. Cook the paste in the oil until it is dry and caramelized, 8 to 10 minutes. Proceed with the recipe, then use the leaves from the cilantro bunch as garnish.

Cheat's Onion Soup

I say *cheat* because this recipe doesn't require a labor-intensive beef broth—also because it contains some of my favorite ways to add umami to vegetarian cooking: miso and tomato paste. The plentiful Parmesan cheese doesn't hurt either.

SERVES 4

¼ cup [60 ml] extra-virgin olive oil

2 lb [910 g] onions, preferably yellow, peeled, halved, and thinly sliced

1 tsp kosher salt, plus more for seasoning

½ tsp freshly ground black pepper, plus more for seasoning

1 Tbsp tomato paste

¼ cup [60 g] yellow or white miso (or red for maximum umami flavor)

4 small bread slices (or 2 large slices, halved)

½ cup [15 g] grated Parmesan cheese

In a large pot over medium-high heat, warm the oil until it shimmers. Add the onions, salt, and pepper and cook, stirring occasionally, until the onions are browned in spots, 5 to 8 minutes. Lower the heat to medium-low so the onions sizzle without burning, and continue cooking until they are soft and golden, another 20 to 25 minutes.

When the onions are ready, add the tomato paste and cook, stirring constantly, long enough to caramelize the tomato paste but before anything on the bottom of the pot burns, 4 to 5 minutes. You don't want the tomato flavor, just the more caramelized notes. Add 4 cups [960 ml] of water and scrape all the good stuff off the bottom of the pan, then bring the mixture to a boil. Remove from the heat and use a ladle to scoop out about ½ cup [120 ml] of the broth and add it to a small bowl with the miso. Whisk the mixture until smooth, then pour it back into the pot. Taste and add more salt and pepper, if you like.

Preheat the broiler and toast the bread until it is golden, 2 to 3 minutes on each side. Scatter the cheese over the bread and return to the broiler. Cook—

watching like a hawk—until the cheese is bubbling and browned in spots, 2 to 3 minutes.

To serve: Ladle the soup into bowls, then float the toast, cheese-side up, on top of each bowl. Eat right away, so the bread doesn't get too soggy.

FRESHEN IT!

—

Add 2 sprigs of thyme to the pot with the onions for even more depth of flavor.

Spicy Noodle Soup

Pantry cooking can sometimes seem like an unsexy topic. You certainly won't see Pasta and Chickpeas (page 90) on the cover of any glossy food magazines. But occasionally, when the stars align and you're all stocked up, you can make something as flavorful, mouthwatering, and special enough for guests as this soup.

SERVES 4

½ large or 1 small onion, any kind, peeled and coarsely chopped

3 garlic cloves, peeled and coarsely chopped

One 2 in [5 cm] piece fresh ginger, peeled and coarsely chopped

2½ tsp kosher salt, plus more for seasoning

4 bone-in, skin-on chicken thighs, fully thawed and patted dry

¼ tsp freshly ground black pepper

1 to 2 tsp red pepper flakes, depending on your affinity for heat

1 tsp ground turmeric

One 14 oz [420 ml] can coconut milk

8 oz [230 g] rice noodles, any thickness (though I prefer them to be thinner)

1 cup [120 g] frozen peas

3 limes, 1 cut into wedges for serving, plus more as needed

cont.

Bring 5 cups [1.2 L] of water to a boil and keep hot. Place the onion, garlic, ginger, and 1 tsp of the salt into a blender with 3 Tbsp of water and purée until smooth. (If you don't have a blender, you can use a mini food processor, mortar and pestle, or put all the ingredients minus the water into a heavy-duty zip-top plastic bag and bash it with a rolling pin until it becomes a paste.)

Season the chicken with ½ tsp of the salt and the black pepper. In a large pot over medium-high heat, add the chicken skin-side down and cook, undisturbed, until the skin is a deep golden color and doesn't stick to the pan, 8 to 10 minutes. Flip the chicken and continue cooking until the other side is well browned and the chicken is mostly cooked through, 5 to 7 minutes. Transfer the chicken to a cutting board to cool.

cont.

pantry to plate

OPTIONAL ADDITIONS

4 oz [115 g] tofu, drained (see page 120) and cut into 1 in [2.5 cm] pieces

1 cup [60 g] thinly sliced cabbage

2 hard-boiled eggs, halved (see page 32)

Return the pot to medium heat. Add the seasoning paste, red pepper flakes, and turmeric to the pot and cook, stirring constantly and scraping up the good stuff from the bottom of the pan, until it is dry and caramelized, 5 to 7 minutes. Pour in the coconut milk and 4 cups [960 ml] of water and bring the mixture to a boil. Lower the heat so it simmers gently and let the soup cook while you prepare the rest of the ingredients.

In a large heatproof bowl, cover the noodles with the reserved hot water and soak until they are pliable (timing will depend on the thickness and brand; read the directions on the package). Drain the noodles and rinse with cold water, then let drain in a colander.

Remove the skin and bones from the chicken and discard. Chop the meat into bite-size pieces (don't worry if the chicken is still a little pink, as it will cook more in the next step).

Add the peas and chicken to the simmering broth and cook until warmed through. Remove from the heat and add the juice of two of the limes and the remaining 1 tsp of salt. Taste the soup and add more salt or lime juice, if you like. Divide the noodles among four bowls, pour the soup over the noodles, top with any optional additions, if using, and serve right away. (If not eating immediately, store the rice noodles separately.)

FRESHEN IT!
—

Instead of half an onion and red pepper flakes, use 2 peeled shallots and 1 fresh chile, like a Fresno or serrano (seeds removed, if you like). Garnish the soup with lots of chopped fresh cilantro.

A GIFT TO YOURSELF

◇◇◇◇◇

Most of the soup recipes in this book (and all the other recipes, actually) make four generous servings. If you're cooking for a family, that's a convenient amount. If you live alone, or with one other person, it can seem like . . . too much. So when you've eaten the same soup for three meals in a row and can't take it anymore, divide any remaining soup into individual portion containers and freeze. Think of them as a gift to your future self. You'll have an easy lunch or dinner ready to thaw when you can stand the thought of that particular recipe again—just make sure it's no more than 6 months later (see A Note on Storage on page 17).

Black Bean Soup

Here's a classic bean soup that's comforting on its own, and a downright fun DIY meal when served with as many garnishes as you can scrounge up. I included yogurt (in place of sour cream) and lime wedges, but you can add minced onion, thinly sliced cabbage, or even homemade tortilla chips (see the directions on page 34). There isn't enough cooking time for this quick soup to develop a rich broth—that comes from dried beans—but by blending everything together (plus some flavorful additions like tomato paste and chipotle peppers), you'll have a very tasty bowlful.

SERVES 4

3 Tbsp vegetable oil

1 onion, any kind, peeled and chopped

3 garlic cloves, peeled and chopped

1 carrot, peeled and chopped

1 tsp kosher salt, plus more for seasoning

½ tsp freshly ground black pepper

2 Tbsp tomato paste

1 tsp ground cumin

Two 14 oz [400 g] cans black beans, drained and rinsed

2 chipotle peppers in adobo sauce, or to taste, plus more sauce for seasoning

3 limes, 1 cut into wedges for garnish

Greek yogurt, for garnish

In a large pot over medium-high heat, warm the oil until it shimmers. Add the onion, garlic, and carrot and season with the salt and black pepper. Cook, stirring often and lowering the heat if the onion starts to burn, until the onion is soft and golden, 8 to 10 minutes. Add the tomato paste and cook, stirring constantly, long enough to cook the tomato paste but before anything on the bottom of the pot burns, about 1 minute. Add the cumin and cook, stirring constantly, until fragrant, less than 1 minute.

Add the beans, chipotle peppers, and 5 cups [1.2 L] of water to the pot and bring to a boil. Lower the heat so the soup simmers steadily and cook for as long as you can to allow the flavors to come together, at least 15 minutes and up to 30 minutes if you have the time/patience. Turn off the heat, add the juice of 2 limes, and stir. Taste, then add more salt and/or adobo sauce, if you like.

Use a handheld blender to purée the soup directly in the pot—blend for at least 2 minutes to get the soup as smooth as possible. If you don't have a handheld blender: Let the soup cool slightly and, very carefully, transfer the soup in batches to a blender or—in a pinch—food processor, and purée until smooth. If using a regular blender, leave a gap between part of the lid and the blender that's large enough to let steam escape but small enough so that hot soup doesn't splash out and burn you, and never fill the blender more than halfway full.

Transfer the soup to a clean pot and bring it back to a boil. Serve hot, garnished with yogurt and with lime wedges on the side.

FRESHEN IT!

To pack more vegetable content into your soup, add 1 cored and chopped red bell pepper with the onion and carrot, and garnish with avocado slices and chopped fresh cilantro.

Ribollita

I love a soup that's a mix of some chopped aromatics combined with the contents of a few cans. I *especially* love a soup when I can add something straight from the freezer. It's so very convenient for lazy cooks like myself. This soup gets better with age, but leave the bread out if you're not serving the soup the day it's made.

SERVES 4 TO 6

¼ cup [60 ml] extra-virgin olive oil

3 celery stalks, chopped

2 carrots, peeled and chopped

1 onion, any kind, peeled and chopped

4 garlic cloves, peeled and sliced

1 tsp kosher salt, plus more for seasoning

1 tsp freshly ground black pepper, plus more for seasoning

One 28 oz [800 g] can whole tomatoes

One 14 oz [400 g] can chickpeas, drained and rinsed

One 10 oz [280 g] bag frozen greens

¼ to ½ tsp red pepper flakes, depending on your affinity for heat

4 oz [115 g] sliced crusty bread, thawed if necessary

½ cup [15 g] grated Parmesan cheese, for serving

In a large pot over medium-high heat, warm the oil until it shimmers. Add the celery, carrots, onion, and garlic and season with the salt and black pepper. Cook, stirring often and lowering the heat if the onion starts to burn, until the onion is soft, 8 to 10 minutes. Add the tomatoes and their juices and, using your spoon, break up the tomatoes.

Add the chickpeas, greens, red pepper flakes, and 4 cups [960 ml] of water and bring the mixture to a boil. Lower the heat so the mixture simmers gently and cook, uncovered and stirring occasionally, until the carrots are tender, 25 to 30 minutes, or for up to 45 minutes if you've got the time. Taste the soup and add more salt and black pepper, if you like.

Tear the bread into bite-size pieces and add it to the simmering soup. Cook, stirring once or twice, until the bread is just saturated, 3 to 5 minutes. Ladle the soup into bowls, top with the cheese, and serve right away.

FRESHEN IT!

In place of the frozen greens, use 1 head of fresh bitter greens, like escarole or frisée, chopped, and add it with the bread so it just wilts.

Chickpea Potato Soup

I *love* this soup. I cannot give it a hearty (pun intended) enough recommendation. Just make sure you're feeling a little chilled when you make it and you don't plan on leaving your home again for the night, because everything is about to get very cozy.

SERVES 4

2 Tbsp butter

2 Tbsp extra-virgin olive oil, plus more for garnish

1 yellow onion, peeled, halved, and thinly sliced

1 tsp kosher salt, plus more for seasoning

1 tsp black peppercorns, crushed, plus more for seasoning

Two 14 oz [400 g] cans chickpeas, drained and rinsed

1 large all-purpose potato like Yukon gold, peeled and cut into ½ in [12 mm] cubes

½ cup [15 g] grated Parmesan cheese

FRESHEN IT!
—
Swap in 2 cleaned and chopped leeks for the onion, and add 1 bunch of fresh escarole, chopped, with the chickpeas.

In a large pot over medium-high heat, warm the butter and oil until the butter melts. Add the onion and season with the salt and pepper. Cook, stirring often and lowering the heat if the onion starts to burn, until the onion is soft and golden, 8 to 10 minutes.

Add the chickpeas, potato, and 5 cups [1.2 L] of water and bring to a boil. Lower the heat so the soup simmers gently and cook until the potatoes are very tender, 20 to 25 minutes. Remove the soup from the heat and taste; add more salt and pepper, if you like.

Use a handheld blender to purée the soup directly in the pot until about half of the soup is smooth—so it's both creamy and chunky. If you don't have a handheld blender, use a potato masher or a wooden spoon and some elbow grease to mash about half the soup.

Ladle the soup into bowls and top with a generous amount of grated Parmesan cheese and a splash of olive oil and serve hot.

Tortilla Soup with Chicken

You can't go wrong with a spicy, bright broth and fried tortillas, right? This soup is also a great vehicle for any leftover beans, roasted vegetables, or greens you have in your fridge to make it even heartier.

SERVES 4

4 bone-in, skin-on chicken thighs, fully thawed and patted dry

2 tsp kosher salt, plus more for seasoning

½ tsp freshly ground black pepper, plus more for seasoning

1 onion, any kind, peeled and chopped

2 garlic cloves, peeled and sliced

3 Tbsp tomato paste

1 tsp ground cumin

1 chipotle pepper in adobo sauce, with some adobo sauce if you like

One 14 oz [400 g] can black beans, drained and rinsed

4 canned whole tomatoes, chopped or squeezed into bite-size pieces

¼ cup [60 ml] vegetable oil

4 tortillas, cut into bite-size strips

cont.

Place the chicken thighs skin-side up on a cutting board or plate and season with 1 tsp of the salt and the black pepper. Warm a large pot over medium-high heat, then add the chicken, skin-side down, in a single layer and let it cook, undisturbed, until the skin is golden brown and doesn't stick to the pan, 8 to 10 minutes. Flip the chicken and continue cooking until the other side is well browned and the chicken is mostly cooked through, 5 to 7 minutes. Transfer the chicken to a cutting board.

Add the onion, garlic, and remaining 1 tsp of salt to the pot. Cook, stirring to scrape up the good stuff from the bottom of the pot, until the onion starts to turn golden, 8 to 10 minutes. Add the tomato paste, cumin, and chipotle pepper and cook, stirring constantly and mashing the pepper with your spoon, long enough to cook the tomato paste but before anything on the bottom of the pot burns, about 1 minute.

cont.

3 limes, 1 cut into wedges for garnish

¼ cup [30 g] crumbled queso fresco or feta cheese

Greek yogurt, for serving

Pour in 8 cups [2 L] of water, the beans, and tomatoes and return the chicken to the pot. Bring the mixture to a boil, uncovered, then lower the heat so it simmers steadily. While the chicken cooks, use a large spoon to carefully skim off any foam that rises to the top of the pot. Continue cooking and let the stock simmer and reduce while you make the tortilla strips.

In a large skillet over medium-high heat, warm the oil until it shimmers. Add the tortillas and cook, stirring constantly to keep them from sticking together, until golden and crisp, 4 to 5 minutes. Transfer to a paper towel–lined plate to drain and season with a big pinch of salt.

Remove the chicken from the pot and discard the skin and bones. Use two forks to shred the cooked chicken and divide it between four serving bowls, then top with the tortilla strips. Cut the two whole limes in half and squeeze the juice into the broth. Taste and add more salt and black pepper, if you like. Ladle the soup over the chicken, then top with the cheese and dollop with the yogurt. Serve hot, with lime wedges as a garnish.

FRESHEN IT!
—

Amp up the garnishes: Use 4 thinly sliced radishes, diced avocado, and chopped fresh cilantro.

Chicken Noodle Soup

A soup for a very specific mood: When you're craving comfort but you don't have time to make the real deal, nor do you want to leave home. So this version—which is close to the classic while cutting serious time—will scratch that itch. Browning the chicken skin and the squeeze of lemon at the end gives the flavor some oomph, and you get dinner about as quickly as homemade soup can be made (which is still, after all, *some* time).

SERVES 3 TO 4

4 bone-in, skin-on chicken thighs, fully thawed and patted dry

2 tsp kosher salt, plus more for seasoning

½ tsp freshly ground black pepper, plus more for seasoning

2 celery stalks, chopped, and leaves reserved if you've still got them

2 carrots, peeled and chopped

1 onion, preferably yellow, peeled and chopped

½ cup [60 g] macaroni or other short pasta

½ lemon

Place the chicken thighs skin-side up on a cutting board or plate and season with 1 tsp of the salt and the pepper. Heat a large pot over medium-high heat. Add the chicken, skin-side down, in a single layer and let it cook, undisturbed, until the skin is golden brown and doesn't stick to the pot, 8 to 10 minutes. Transfer the chicken to a plate, and add the celery, carrots, and onion to the pot. Cook, stirring to scrape up the good stuff from the bottom of the pot, until the onion is soft but not yet taking on any color, 8 to 10 minutes.

Pour in 8 cups [2 L] of water and add the remaining 1 tsp of salt and the chicken. Bring the mixture to a boil, uncovered. While the chicken cooks, use a large spoon to carefully skim off any foam that rises to the top of the pot. Continue cooking until the chicken is cooked through and no longer pink, 10 to 15 minutes. Remove the chicken and transfer it to a plate to cool.

Add the macaroni to the pot and cook, stirring occasionally, until it is al dente, a.k.a. pleasantly bouncy and not mushy, 6 to 8 minutes. Remove the pot from the heat. Discard the chicken skin and bones and shred the meat with two forks. Add it to the pot along with any juices that have accumulated on the plate. Squeeze in the lemon half and taste, adding more salt or pepper, if you like. Garnish with the celery leaves if you have them and serve right away. (If you aren't planning on eating the soup immediately, cook the pasta in a separate pot according to the package directions and add it to the soup just before serving.)

FRESHEN IT!

Something green always makes soups feel more satisfying for me. Try adding 8 oz [230 g] of fresh spinach in the last few minutes of cooking or 8 oz [230 g] of chopped kale with the macaroni. In the summer, the kernels from 2 ears of fresh corn and 2 chopped zucchini would be a very nice addition.

Carbs (Rice *and* Pasta)

A category that's often vilified, carbs are the workhorses of the pantry and definitely belong in yours. Besides being delicious and filling, they're super budget friendly. You can always bulk up the sides you're making to rely less on pure carbs to fill you up—and then you'll have plenty of leftovers. Might I suggest the Leftovers Frittata recipe on page 43?

Plain White Rice

You need to know how to make a pot of (white) rice for many of the recipes in this chapter and in life, generally. So, here's a handy guide for you to learn the art of perfect rice.

MAKES 4½ CUPS [540 G]

1½ cups [300 g] long-grain white rice

1 tsp kosher salt

In a small pot with a tight-fitting lid, cover the rice with water and swirl it with your hands until the water is cloudy, taking care not to break any of the grains. Drain the rice into a colander and repeat until the water is clear. Shake off as much water as you can from the rice and transfer it back to the pot. Wrap the lid with a dish towel and securely knot the towel on top of the lid so the corners won't reach down into your stove's flame.

Add 3 cups [720 ml] of water to the pot along with the salt and bring to a boil, uncovered, over medium-high heat. Lower the heat so the water simmers gently and cook, undisturbed, until the surface of the rice looks dry and holes appear, 5 to 8 minutes. Turn the heat to very low, place the cloth-wrapped lid on the pot, and cook for 10 minutes. Remove from the heat and let sit, covered and undisturbed, for 10 minutes.

Use a fork to separate the grains (this is what "fluffing" means) and serve, or let cool in the refrigerator to use later (like for fried rice).

FOR COOLING QUICKLY: Spread the rice on the largest baking sheet or plate that will fit in your refrigerator; the more surface area, the quicker it will cool. Place the sheet into the refrigerator and leave to cool for as long as possible, or up to overnight. Cooling allows the grains to separate, which means each one will get toasty and fried.

Basic Fried Rice

Fried rice is a (delicious) technique for using up leftover rice. Thus, to make it, you must have leftover rice. The best way to do this is to make a batch of Plain White Rice (facing page) the night before you want fried rice. But we can't have so much foresight all the time, so the quick-cool technique on the facing page comes in handy. You can use it for any grains, really, if you need to cool them quickly to make a salad or pack lunch, say.

For the actual fried rice technique, make sure your pan is very, very hot before adding ingredients to ensure they don't steam and get mushy—the enemy of a good fried rice.

SERVES 4

4 Tbsp [60 ml] vegetable oil

½ onion, any kind, peeled and chopped

2 carrots, peeled and chopped

2 cups [300 g] frozen broccoli, thawed, blotted dry if necessary, and chopped

3 large eggs, whisked

½ tsp kosher salt

¼ tsp freshly ground black pepper

2 garlic cloves, peeled and minced

One 1 in [2.5 cm] piece fresh ginger, peeled and minced

1 batch Plain White Rice (facing page)

1 cup [120 g] frozen peas, thawed, blotted dry if necessary

2 Tbsp soy sauce, plus more for seasoning

1 lime, cut into wedges, for serving

In a large cast-iron or other heavy-duty skillet (just not nonstick) over high heat, warm 2 Tbsp of the oil until it shimmers. Add the onion and carrots and cook, stirring as little as possible, until the vegetables are charred in spots, 2 to 3 minutes. Use a slotted spoon to transfer the vegetables to a bowl, leaving the oil in the skillet. Repeat with the broccoli, cooking undisturbed until it is well browned on one side, another 2 to 3 minutes. Transfer to the bowl with the vegetables.

Remove the skillet from the heat, add the eggs, and season with the salt and pepper. Cook, stirring constantly to break up the eggs, until they are just barely cooked and still slightly runny (don't worry, they'll cook more), less than 1 minute. Transfer to the bowl with the other cooked ingredients.

cont.

Return the skillet to the heat, let it get really hot, and add the remaining 2 Tbsp of oil. Add the garlic and ginger and cook just until fragrant, 30 seconds or less. Add the rice and cook, stirring every 10 seconds or so, until the rice is browned in spots, 2 to 3 minutes total.

Return the cooked ingredients to the skillet along with the peas and soy sauce and toss to combine. Cook until everything is hot, 1 to 2 minutes. Remove from the heat, taste, and add more soy sauce, if you like. Serve hot, with the lime wedges on the side.

FRESHEN IT!

Add up to 2 cups [about 260 g] more chopped vegetables to the dish; cook until they are charred in spots but still crisp, 1 to 3 minutes, depending on the vegetable. A small selection of vegetables that would be delicious: snap peas, bell peppers, any sturdy green, cauliflower, scallions, corn kernels (no more than 1 cup [140 g]), or thinly sliced cabbage.

Crispy Rice Cake with Greens

This is a riff on one of my favorite dishes—a golden Persian rice cake called *tachin*. I took it in an Italian direction, however, since saffron and barberries didn't make the cut for this book's pantry list. If you have a rotisserie chicken or some leftover cooked vegetables, you could substitute those ingredients for the filling and cut down on prep time.

SERVES 6

⅓ cup [80 ml] plus 3 Tbsp vegetable oil

1 onion, preferably yellow, peeled and chopped

2 garlic cloves, peeled and minced

2 Tbsp plus 2 tsp kosher salt

One 10 oz [280 g] bag frozen greens (kale is very nice here)

2 cups [400 g] long-grain white rice

1½ cups [360 g] Greek yogurt

3 large egg yolks

½ cup [15 g] grated Parmesan cheese

In a large skillet over medium-high heat, warm 2 Tbsp of the oil until it shimmers. Add the onion, garlic, and 1 tsp of the salt. Cook, stirring occasionally, until the onion is soft and golden, 8 to 10 minutes. Add the greens and cook, stirring constantly, until the greens are warmed through, 2 to 3 minutes. Remove from the heat and reserve, draining off any excess liquid.

Preheat the oven to 400°F [200°C]. Fill a large pot with water and bring it to a boil, then add 2 Tbsp of the salt. Add the rice to the boiling water and stir to prevent the rice from sticking to the bottom of the pot. Cook the rice, stirring occasionally, until it is tender on the outside but still has some bite in the center, 6 to 8 minutes. Drain the rice and rinse with cold water to stop the cooking.

In a large bowl, mix together the yogurt, ⅓ cup [80 ml] of the oil, the egg yolks, cheese, and the remaining 1 tsp of salt. Add the rice to the bowl and mix, very gently and using a spatula, until the rice is fully coated. Oil a 9 in [23 cm] square baking pan with the remaining 1 Tbsp of vegetable oil. Spread half of the rice mixture into the pan and smooth the top. Then add the greens and smooth them as well. Top with the remaining rice mixture and gently smooth the top.

Cover the baking pan with aluminum foil and transfer it to the oven. Bake until the edges are golden brown, 55 to 65 minutes. Remove the pan from the oven and let the cake sit for 10 minutes, then remove the foil and invert the cake onto a serving platter (see the directions on page 42 for guidance on the flipping technique, but don't put the cake back into the pan). Cut the cake into slices and serve.

FRESHEN IT!
—

Not a fresh vegetable, but this dish is greatly improved by the addition of dried fruit. Sauté ¼ cup [35 g] of raisins and an equal amount of pine nuts with the onions and garlic before adding the greens to the pan.

Chicken Paella-ish

Is this made with bomba rice over a grill? No. Would a Spaniard call this paella? Probably not. Is it a delicious, satisfying weeknight dinner? Absolutely.

SERVES 4

4 bone-in, skin-on chicken thighs, fully thawed and patted dry

1 tsp kosher salt

1 onion, any kind, peeled and chopped

2 Tbsp tomato paste

1½ tsp paprika, sweet or hot

¼ tsp ground turmeric

1 cup [200 g] long-grain white rice, rinsed (see page 72)

1 cup [120 g] frozen peas

Place the chicken on a cutting board skin-side up and season with the salt. In a large skillet over medium-high heat, place the chicken skin-side down and cook, undisturbed, until the skin is golden brown and doesn't stick to the skillet, 8 to 10 minutes. Flip the chicken and continue cooking until the other side is well browned and the chicken is mostly cooked through, 5 to 7 minutes. Transfer the chicken to a plate.

Add the onion to the skillet and cook, stirring to scrape up the good stuff from the bottom of the skillet, until the onion starts to turn golden, 8 to 10 minutes. Add the tomato paste, paprika, and turmeric and continue cooking, stirring constantly, long enough to cook the tomato paste but before anything on the bottom of the pot burns, about 1 minute.

Add the rice to the skillet and stir to coat in the seasoning mixture. Pour in 2 cups [480 ml] of water and bring to a boil. Stir in the peas and then nestle the chicken in the skillet, skin-side up. Lower the heat so the water simmers gently. Cover the skillet and

cont.

pantry to plate

cook until the rice is tender and the chicken is cooked through (you can check by cutting a piece close to the bone and seeing if there is still pink inside), 20 to 25 minutes.

Uncover the skillet and turn the heat up to medium-high. Cook, rotating the skillet a quarter turn every 30 seconds, and keeping a close eye on the skillet, until you can either smell toasted rice or you can hear sizzling, 2 minutes total. Bring the skillet to the table (with something to rest it on, of course) and serve hot, family style.

FRESHEN IT!

Two wonderful and (somewhat) classic additions: 1 red bell pepper, cored and sliced, added to the skillet with the onion; and 2 fresh tomatoes, cut into wedges, nestled on top of the rice with the chicken. Season the tomatoes with a little extra salt so their juices flavor the rice.

Get-Home-Ravenous Noodles

Here's a kind of anything-goes noodle dish that's easy and super satisfying. My starting point was the classic Vietnamese combo of fish sauce and lime, but made vegetarian for times I didn't feel like eating fish or, more accurately, had run out of fish sauce but was starving and needed dinner ASAP. Sometimes moments of desperation produce wonderful ideas.

This makes a great lunch. Just be sure to have a little extra dressing with you—the rice noodles keep absorbing the sauce and they can get a little dry when they're cold.

SERVES 4

One 14 oz [400 g] block tofu, preferably extra-firm, drained (see page 120)

1 tsp kosher salt

¼ tsp freshly ground black pepper

½ cup [120 ml] vegetable oil

8 oz [230 g] dried rice noodles, any thickness

1 cup [120 g] frozen peas

⅓ cup [80 ml] soy sauce

⅓ cup [80 ml] fresh lime juice (from about 3 limes)

1 garlic clove, peeled and smashed

½ to 1 tsp red pepper flakes, depending on your affinity for heat

In a medium pot, bring 5 cups [1.2 L] of water to a boil and set aside. Cut the tofu in half lengthwise, then slice each half perpendicularly to make ½ in [12 mm] thick slices. Spread the slices on paper towels or a clean dish towel and blot both sides dry. Season the tofu with the salt and black pepper.

In the largest nonstick skillet you have over medium-high heat, warm ¼ cup [60 ml] of the oil until it shimmers. Carefully add the tofu in a single layer, making sure each piece has some personal space (meaning they shouldn't all be touching; you may need to work in batches). Cook, undisturbed, until the tofu is a deep golden color on one side, 5 to 6 minutes. Use tongs to flip the tofu and repeat on the other side. Transfer the tofu to paper towels to drain and repeat with the remaining tofu slices, if necessary.

cont.

In a large heatproof bowl, cover the noodles with the boiling water and soak until they are pliable (the timing will depend on the thickness and brand; read the directions on the package). Place the peas in a colander, then drain the noodles over them and shake off any excess water. Transfer everything to a bowl of cold water until ready to serve.

In an 8 oz [240 ml] or bigger clean jar with a tight-fitting lid, combine the soy sauce, lime juice, garlic, red pepper flakes, remaining ¼ cup [60 ml] of oil, and ⅓ cup [80 ml] of water. Seal the jar and shake vigorously to combine.

Drain the noodles and peas, shake off as much water as possible, and transfer them to a large bowl. Add the fried tofu, then pour over half of the dressing. Toss everything to coat and taste a noodle; if you'd like more dressing, go for it. Serve at room temperature.

FRESHEN IT!

This is a dish I want to eat at the height of summer, with the addition of as much fresh cilantro and mint as I can handle—which is a lot. In quantifiable terms, I'd call it 1 cup [12 g] of tender cilantro sprigs and ½ cup [6 g] of fresh mint leaves.

Sesame Noodles

This is the perfect almost-no-cook meal that makes an even better lunch. I usually get sick of anything after eating it as leftovers for 2 days, but this I could eat all week. Just try to have the patience to let the noodles warm up a bit when you take them out of the refrigerator so they're not ice cold. It's hard, but worth it.

SERVES 4

2 Tbsp plus ½ tsp kosher salt, plus more for seasoning

8 oz [230 g] spaghetti

½ cup [110 g] tahini

2 Tbsp white or yellow miso

2 Tbsp vegetable oil

¼ to ½ tsp red pepper flakes, depending on your affinity for heat

One 1 in [2.5 cm] piece fresh ginger, peeled

1 garlic clove, peeled

3 cups [180 g] very thinly sliced cabbage

2 carrots, peeled and cut into matchsticks (see page 46)

Bring a large pot of water to a boil—at least 6 cups [1.4 L]—and mix in 2 Tbsp of the salt. Add the pasta and stir to make sure no noodles stick to the bottom. Cook, stirring occasionally, until the noodles are al dente, a.k.a. pleasantly bouncy and not mushy, 8 to 9 minutes. Scoop out 1 cup [240 ml] of the pasta cooking water, then drain the noodles. Rinse them with cold water, then shake off as much excess water as you can. Let them continue to drain while you make the rest of the dish.

In a small bowl, whisk together the tahini, miso, oil, red pepper flakes, and remaining ½ tsp of salt. Continue whisking and start to pour in—very slowly—the reserved pasta cooking water. The tahini will get very thick, then look chunky, then eventually thin out. Continue adding water until the mixture is the consistency of melted chocolate, about ¾ cup [180 ml] of water total. Use a Microplane to grate in the ginger and garlic, mix, then taste and add more salt, if you like.

Place the noodles in a large bowl, add the cabbage and carrots, and pour about half of the sauce into the bowl. Toss with tongs—carefully so you don't break the pasta—until everything is evenly coated in sauce, then taste. Add as much of the remaining sauce as you like (I love a well-sauced noodle, so no judgment), and serve at room temperature.

FRESHEN IT!

The obvious—and welcome— addition to this dish is 1 English or 2 Persian cucumbers, thinly sliced, and 2 scallions, chopped.

Rich Kimchi Noodles

Kimchi—a pantry staple for millennia—is basically three ingredients in one: crunchy vegetable, seasoning, and cooking liquid. Make sure that whatever brand you buy comes with lots of the brine so you can make these more-delicious-than-they-have-a-right-to-be noodles. If you buy a vegetarian kimchi, you might need to add 1 Tbsp of soy sauce to amp up the savoriness.

These noodles don't store very well, so the recipe is for two servings, but can easily be doubled if you have more mouths to feed.

SERVES 2

4 Tbsp [55 g] butter

1 cup [250 g] chopped kimchi, drained

½ cup [40 g] shredded peeled carrot

½ cup [120 ml] kimchi brine (or as much kimchi brine as you have supplemented with water)

4 oz [115 g] rice noodles, any thickness

FRESHEN IT!
—
We'll keep it simple for this easy dish: Garnish the finished noodles with 2 sliced scallions (green and white parts).

In a small pot, bring 4 cups [960 ml] of water to a boil and set aside. In a large skillet over medium-high heat, melt 2 Tbsp of the butter. As soon as the butter foams, add the kimchi and carrot and cook, stirring often, until it has browned in spots, 3 to 5 minutes. Add the kimchi brine and bring to a boil, then lower the heat to very low and keep warm.

In a large heatproof bowl, cover the rice noodles with the boiling water. Soak the noodles until they are pliable (timing will depend on the thickness and brand; read the directions on the package). Drain the noodles and shake off as much excess water as possible.

Turn the heat back up to medium-high in the skillet and add the noodles and remaining 2 Tbsp of butter. Use tongs to mix the ingredients and toss the noodles until the butter and brine emulsify to make a nice, thick sauce that coats the noodles. Transfer immediately to bowls or plates and serve.

pantry to plate

Not Quite Cacio e Pepe

This simple Italian dish had a moment around 2017, and while some dishes can seem passé after something like that, this technique has staying power. Knowing how to turn pasta and cheese into a meal is like knowing how to shop your own closet or redecorate while spending no money. It's a life skill. But this is "not quite" the dish for a few reasons: First, it doesn't use Pecorino (personally, I think it's too strong and also it didn't make the pantry cut); second, I add butter to help get the sauce nice and emulsified. I'm sure you won't mind.

SERVES 4

2 tsp black peppercorns

2 Tbsp salt

12 oz [340 g] spaghetti or linguine

6 Tbsp [85 g] butter, plus more as needed

1¼ cups [40 g] grated Parmesan cheese

Place the peppercorns in a zip-top plastic bag and bash them with a rolling pin until all the peppercorns are cracked. Reserve for the sauce.

Bring a large pot of water to a boil—at least 6 cups [1.4 L]—and mix in the salt. Add the pasta and stir to make sure no noodles stick to the bottom. Cook, stirring occasionally, until the noodles are al dente, a.k.a. pleasantly bouncy and not mushy, 8 to 9 minutes. Scoop out about 1 cup [240 ml] of the pasta cooking water, then drain the noodles.

Meanwhile, in a large skillet over medium heat, melt the butter, add the peppercorns, and lower the heat so it stays warm but doesn't brown while the pasta cooks.

When the pasta is ready, add it to the skillet along with ¼ cup [60 ml] of the pasta water and turn the heat up to medium. Using tongs or—if you're feeling daring—your upper body strength, toss the pasta and vigorously stir the mixture so the liquid thickens and turns glossy. Congrats, you just emulsified the sauce! Remove the skillet from the heat, add ½ cup [15 g] of the cheese and another ¼ cup [60 ml] of the pasta water, and repeat the process until the cheese is fully mixed into the sauce, adding more pasta water a splash at a time, if necessary, to loosen the sauce. When the sauce is thick and glossy again, add another ½ cup [15 g] of the cheese and ¼ cup [60 ml] of the pasta water and repeat. If at any point the sauce breaks, a.k.a. turns gloppy and the fat separates from the water, add another 1 Tbsp of butter and 2 Tbsp of water and stir vigorously until the sauce comes back together.

Divide the pasta among bowls and garnish with the remaining ¼ cup [10 g] of cheese. Serve right away. This dish is best eaten the day it's made.

FRESHEN IT!
—

This dish should be appreciated in all its simple, cheesy glory. Add some fiber with a side of salad or any sort of simple vegetable steamed and seasoned with garlic and lemon.

Pasta and Chickpeas

If the temperature outside is below a certain threshold, I could eat this for dinner every night. This classic Italian dish is ridiculously easy, filling, and so very delicious. The only adjustment I make to my version here is cooking the chickpeas just a bit before adding them to the dish. I've found that cooking canned chickpeas for the same length of time as the pasta leaves them a little too firm for my taste. In my opinion, if you're going to eat comfort food, it's got to be pleasantly mushy.

SERVES 4

Two 14 oz [400 g] cans chickpeas, drained and rinsed

¼ cup [60 ml] extra-virgin olive oil

3 garlic cloves, peeled and thinly sliced

½ cup [120 g] tomato paste

1 cup (or 4 oz [120 g]) short pasta like macaroni

2 tsp kosher salt

¼ to ½ tsp red pepper flakes, depending on your affinity for heat

Grated Parmesan cheese, for serving

FRESHEN IT!

Honestly, this dish is perfect as is, but some chopped fresh parsley sprinkled over each bowl wouldn't hurt.

Place the chickpeas in a small pot with 4 cups [960 ml] of water. Bring to a boil and cook, uncovered, for 10 minutes. Keep warm.

In a large skillet over medium heat, warm the oil until it shimmers. Add the garlic and cook, paying very close attention, until it starts to color around the edges, about 1 minute. Immediately—this is important to prevent the garlic from burning—add the tomato paste and cook, stirring constantly, long enough to cook the tomato paste but before anything on the bottom of the skillet burns, about 1 minute. Add the pasta, the chickpeas and their cooking liquid, the salt, and red pepper flakes and stir to combine.

Bring the mixture to a boil, then lower the heat so it simmers steadily. Cook, stirring often, until the pasta is cooked, 12 to 15 minutes. Ladle the mixture into bowls, garnish with grated cheese, and serve hot.

Pasta with Yogurt and Caramelized Onions

This recipe is a riff on a wonderful Diane Kochilas recipe I discovered a few years back. Writing this now, I'm wondering why I don't make it every week. And even better: It's forgiving. Burn the onions? That's added flavor. Undercook them? It will be a touch sweeter and you can just add more Parm. Overcook the pasta? It will make it all the more comforting. The only real thing to note is you're looking for some texture with the cheese, so use the biggest holes on a box grater as opposed to a Microplane. Other than that, you're good to go. I'm about to make a batch now.

SERVES 4

3 Tbsp extra-virgin olive oil

2 large onions, any kind, peeled, halved, and thinly sliced

2 Tbsp plus 1 tsp kosher salt

12 oz [340 g] spaghetti or linguine

1 cup [240 g] Greek yogurt

½ tsp freshly ground black pepper

1 cup [30 g] coarsely grated Parmesan cheese

Fill the largest pot you have with at least 6 cups [1.4 L] of water and place it over high heat, covered, to boil.

Meanwhile, in a large skillet over medium-high heat, warm the oil until it shimmers. Add the onions and 1 tsp of the salt. Once the onions release most of their liquid—3 to 5 minutes—lower the heat to medium. Cook, stirring often and lowering the heat if the onions darken too quickly, until the onions are a golden brown, at least 30 minutes and, if you have the patience, up to 45 minutes.

When the water boils, add the remaining 2 Tbsp of salt to the pot. Add the pasta and stir to make sure no noodles stick to the bottom. Cook, stirring occasionally, until the noodles are al dente, a.k.a. pleasantly bouncy and not mushy, 8 to 9 minutes.

Scoop out about 1 cup [240 ml] of the pasta cooking water, then drain the noodles.

In a large serving bowl, mix together the pasta, caramelized onions, Greek yogurt, and pepper. Use tongs or two forks to gently toss everything together, adding the pasta cooking water a splash at a time to loosen the yogurt. You're not looking for a sauce, but you'll need at least ¼ cup [60 ml] of the water so the yogurt evenly coats the noodles. Garnish with half of the cheese, then serve hot, letting people add more cheese if they'd like.

FRESHEN IT!

You could go two directions here: One bunch of curly kale, chopped and added to the pasta cooking water for the last 5 minutes would turn the pasta into a whole meal, as would 1 lb [455 g] of cherry tomatoes roasted in a 400°F [200°C] oven until nice and caramelized and then tossed into the pasta with the final ingredients.

Spaghetti with Tomato Sauce

I get wary of a cookbook that tells you all processed foods are bad and everything should be homemade. Anyone with a full-time job (or a part-time job or a family or some combination) knows sometimes you have to take shortcuts in the kitchen. And there are some legitimately very good jarred tomato sauces available. *My* issue with them is that they're expensive. You can have a delicious tomato sauce in 45 minutes—it takes 20 minutes to boil a pot of water for pasta anyway—and that's my main reason for cooking it from scratch. And that it tastes delicious, obviously.

SERVES 4

¼ cup [60 ml] extra-virgin olive oil

½ large or 1 small onion, any kind, peeled and minced

2 garlic cloves, peeled and thinly sliced

2 Tbsp plus 1 tsp kosher salt

¼ to ½ tsp red pepper flakes, depending on your affinity for heat

2 Tbsp tomato paste (optional)

One 28 oz [800 g] can whole tomatoes

1 tsp grated lemon zest

12 oz [340 g] spaghetti or any long pasta

½ cup [15 g] grated Parmesan cheese

Fill the largest pot you have with water—at least 6 cups [1.4 L]—cover it, and place it over high heat to boil.

Meanwhile, in a large skillet over medium-high heat, warm the oil until it shimmers. Add the onion, garlic, and 1 tsp of the salt and cook, stirring often and lowering the heat if the onions start to brown, until the onions are a light golden color, 8 to 10 minutes.

Add the red pepper flakes and tomato paste, if using, and cook for about 30 seconds, then pour in the tomatoes and their juices. Add ½ cup [120 ml] of water to the can, capturing any tomato sticking to the sides, and add it to the skillet. Bring the sauce to a boil,

cont.

then lower the heat so it simmers steadily and cook, stirring occasionally and breaking up the tomatoes with your spoon as they cook, until the tomatoes have fallen apart and the sauce has thickened, 20 to 25 minutes. Stir in the lemon zest and taste the sauce, adding more of any of the seasonings, if you like. Turn the heat to very low and cover.

When the sauce has been simmering for 15 minutes or so, add the remaining 2 Tbsp of salt to the boiling water. Add the pasta and stir to make sure no noodles stick to the bottom of the pot. Cook, stirring occasionally, until the noodles are al dente, a.k.a. pleasantly bouncy and not mushy, 8 to 9 minutes. Scoop out about 1 cup [240 ml] of the pasta cooking water, then drain the noodles.

Turn the heat up to medium-high under the sauce and add the spaghetti to the skillet. Use tongs to mix the pasta and sauce, adding the pasta cooking water a splash at a time to help loosen the sauce. You don't want the sauce to be runny, just thinned out enough so it evenly coats the noodles.

Divide the pasta among four plates, garnish with the Parmesan, and serve hot.

FRESHEN IT!

For more—and extra tomatoey—sauce, add 1 pint [440 g] of whole cherry or grape tomatoes to the largest skillet you have when the onions are ready and cook until they've started to burst, 2 to 3 minutes, then proceed with the recipe.

Spicy Tuna Pasta

A box of pasta and a can of tuna in the cupboard are probably what a lot of people picture when they hear "pantry cooking." So here I combine them, with lots of flavorful additions for a bright (thanks to the lemon zest) but hearty year-round dish.

SERVES 4

2 Tbsp extra-virgin olive oil

2 garlic cloves, peeled and thinly sliced

½ to 1 tsp red pepper flakes, depending on your affinity for heat

One 14 oz [400 g] can whole tomatoes, or half of a 28 oz [800 g] can

2 Tbsp plus ½ tsp kosher salt

½ cup [70 g] olives, pitted and chopped

12 oz [340 g] any pasta

Two 6 oz [170 g] cans tuna, preferably packed in oil

1 tsp grated lemon zest

Fill the largest pot you have with water—at least 6 cups [1.4 L]—cover it, and place it over high heat to boil.

In a large skillet over medium heat, warm the oil until it shimmers. Add the garlic and cook, paying very close attention, until it starts to color around the edges, 2 to 3 minutes. Add the red pepper flakes, cook for 10 seconds, then add the tomatoes, the liquid from the can, and ½ tsp of the salt. Use a spoon to break up the tomatoes into bite-size pieces. Bring the mixture to a boil, then lower the heat so it simmers steadily. Add the olives, cover, and cook, stirring occasionally, while you make the pasta.

When the water boils, add the remaining 2 Tbsp of salt, then the pasta. Cook, stirring occasionally so the pasta doesn't stick to the bottom of the pot, until the pasta is al dente, a.k.a. pleasantly bouncy and not mushy, 8 to 9 minutes. Scoop out about ½ cup [120 ml] of the pasta water, then drain the pasta.

cont.

Uncover the tomato sauce and turn the heat back up to medium-high. Add the pasta, tuna, and lemon zest and cook, tossing and adding a splash of the pasta water so the sauce evenly coats the pasta, until the pasta is fully cooked, 4 to 5 minutes. Transfer the finished dish to serving bowls and serve hot.

FRESHEN IT!
—

Finely chop 1 small fennel bulb and add it to the oil before the garlic. Cook, stirring occasionally, until it is browned in spots and has softened, 8 to 10 minutes. Add the garlic and proceed with the recipe.

Pasta with Broccoli and Sausage

Easy, fast, filling, and—perhaps most importantly—a crowd-pleaser.

SERVES 4

2 Tbsp plus ½ tsp kosher salt

12 oz [340 g] short pasta like rigatoni or penne

One 10 oz [280 g] bag frozen broccoli

8 oz [230 g] Italian sausage (hot or sweet), fully thawed and casings removed

1 cup [30 g] grated Parmesan cheese

½ tsp freshly ground black pepper

Red pepper flakes, for garnish

Bring a large pot of water to a boil—at least 6 cups [1.4 L]—and stir in 2 Tbsp of the salt. Add the pasta and stir to make sure no noodles stick to the bottom of the pot. Cook, stirring occasionally, until the noodles are very al dente, a.k.a. still solid in the very center, 7 to 8 minutes. Scoop out 1 cup [240 ml] of the pasta cooking water, then add the broccoli to the pot. Cook until the broccoli has just thawed and is bright green, about 2 minutes. Drain the pasta and broccoli into a colander and shake off the excess water.

Wipe the pot clean and return it to medium-high heat. Use your hands to break up the sausage into pieces as you add it to the pot. Cook, breaking up the sausage more with your spoon, until it is cooked through and browned, 5 to 7 minutes.

cont.

Pour in the reserved cooking water and add the pasta, the broccoli, the cheese, the remaining ½ tsp of salt, and the black pepper. Bring the mixture to a boil and cook, stirring constantly, until the pasta is cooked and the water and cheese have made a glossy sauce, 2 to 3 minutes. Garnish with the red pepper flakes and serve right away.

FRESHEN IT!

Turn it into sausage-and-peppers pasta by cooking 2 red or yellow bell peppers until soft in the pot before adding the sausage. Garnish with lots of parsley.

Beans Are Your *BFF*

As with carbs, beans are cheap, filling, and ridiculously easy to keep on hand. Here, lentils, black beans, chickpeas, and tofu are the starting points for many delicious meals that run the gamut from veggie burgers to a meaty stew.

Not Your Average Beans on Toast

A Mediterranean spin on the British classic that's browned and crisp in all the right places. It's also super easy to make. If you happen to have other types of beans on hand—white beans, gigantes, pinto beans, kidney beans—they all work wonderfully here too. Serve it with some vegetables on the side or with a dish from the egg chapter (page 20) for a complete meal.

SERVES 4

4 Tbsp [60 ml] extra-virgin olive oil

⅓ cup [80 g] tomato paste

1 tsp kosher salt

1 tsp paprika, sweet or hot

¼ tsp freshly ground black pepper

Two 14 oz [400 g] cans chickpeas, drained and rinsed

½ cup [60 g] crumbled feta or queso fresco

4 slices crusty bread, fully thawed

1 garlic clove, peeled

Preheat the broiler. Place the top rack about 4 in [10 cm] away from the heat source.

In a large ovenproof skillet over medium-high heat, warm 3 Tbsp of the oil until it shimmers. Add the tomato paste, salt, paprika, and pepper. Cook, stirring constantly, long enough to cook the tomato paste but before anything on the bottom of the skillet burns, about 1 minute.

Add the chickpeas and 1½ cups [360 ml] of water to the skillet and stir to combine. Carefully transfer the skillet to the rack under the broiler. Cook, watching vigilantly and shaking the skillet a few times, until the water has cooked down and the mixture is saucy, anywhere from 5 to 20 minutes, depending on your broiler. Using oven mitts, pull the rack out, then scatter the cheese over the surface of the mixture and

cont.

pantry to plate

push the rack back in. Continue broiling, watching very carefully now, until the cheese is browned in spots, 2 to 5 minutes. Remove the skillet from the broiler.

Place the bread on the broiler rack and toast, flipping once, until crisp and well browned on both sides, 3 to 5 minutes per side. (You could also use a toaster.) Remove the bread and transfer to a plate, then rub each slice with the garlic clove and drizzle with the remaining 1 Tbsp of oil. Serve family style, or scoop the beans over the toast and serve.

FRESHEN IT!

Thinly slice 8 oz [230 g] of cleaned button mushrooms. Add them to the skillet with the oil before the tomato paste and cook, covered, until they've released all of their water, 5 to 6 minutes. Then uncover and cook, undisturbed, until the skillet is dry and the mushrooms have browned on one side, another 5 to 10 minutes. Add the tomato paste and continue with the recipe. Garnish with chopped fresh cilantro, if you like.

Koshari

The Egyptian classic calls for nearly all the staple carbohydrates to be cooked in one delicious meal. Koshari can include—in addition to everything below—pasta, vermicelli, and a spicy tomato sauce. I've streamlined it for the sake of stove space and time.

SERVES 4

2 Tbsp extra-virgin olive oil

3 large onions, any kind, peeled and thinly sliced

2½ tsp kosher salt

1 cup [200 g] brown or green lentils, rinsed

1½ cups [300 g] long-grain white rice, rinsed (see page 72)

One 14 oz [400 g] can chickpeas, drained and rinsed

½ tsp ground cumin

½ tsp freshly ground black pepper

Paprika, for garnish

1 lemon, cut into quarters, for garnish

FRESHEN IT!
—

There are not really any vegetables in the above recipe. Your best bet is to add one 10 oz [280 g] bag of fresh baby spinach to the pot when you steam the rice and stir to incorporate. Done.

In a large skillet over medium heat, warm the oil until it shimmers. Add the onions and 1 tsp of the salt. Cook, stirring occasionally and lowering the heat if the onions start to brown, until the onions are jammy and golden, 30 to 40 minutes.

Meanwhile, in a large pot, cover the lentils with at least 2 in [5 cm] of water. Bring to a boil, then lower the heat so the water simmers gently. Cook for 10 minutes. Drain the lentils, then return them to the pot with 4 cups [960 ml] of water, the rice, chickpeas, the remaining 1½ tsp of salt, the cumin, and pepper.

Return to a boil, then lower the heat so it simmers gently. Cook, covered, until all the water has been absorbed and the rice is cooked through, 10 to 12 minutes. Turn off the heat, cover, and let the rice steam for 10 minutes. Taste a lentil and if they need a little more time, steam for another 5 minutes.

Fluff the mixture with a fork, then divide among four bowls and top each with a spoonful of caramelized onions. Dust each bowl with paprika, garnish with a lemon wedge, and serve.

Curried Chickpeas

This recipe is a riff on *chana aloo*, the Trinidadian stew that's often stuffed into a roti, or eaten with a roti on the side. It's a perfect dinner, but if you don't have a Caribbean bakery close by, chapati or paratha are great substitutes for the roti, as is the always-available Plain White Rice (page 72).

SERVES 4

3 Tbsp vegetable oil

1 onion, preferably yellow, peeled and chopped

3 garlic cloves, peeled and minced

One 2 in [5 cm] piece fresh ginger, peeled and minced

1½ tsp kosher salt, plus more for seasoning

Two 14 oz [400 g] cans chickpeas, drained and rinsed

1 tsp ground turmeric

½ tsp ground cumin

½ tsp red pepper flakes

½ tsp freshly ground black pepper

1 large baking potato (like russet), peeled and cut into 1 in [2.5 cm] chunks

In a large pot over medium-high heat, warm the oil until it shimmers. Add the onion, garlic, ginger, and salt. Cook, stirring often and lowering the heat if the onion starts to burn, until the onion is soft and golden, 8 to 10 minutes.

Add the chickpeas, turmeric, cumin, red pepper flakes, and black pepper and cook, stirring constantly, until the spices are toasted and fragrant, about 30 seconds. Pour in 2 cups [480 ml] of water and add the potatoes. Bring the mixture to a boil, then lower the heat so it simmers gently. Cook, uncovered, until the potatoes are tender, 20 to 25 minutes. Taste, add more salt, if you like, and serve hot.

FRESHEN IT!
—
To give the stew a brighter flavor, omit the onion and red pepper flakes. Place 1 bunch of cilantro into a blender with ¼ cup [60 ml] of water, half of a seeded habanero pepper (or to taste), and the garlic, ginger, and salt. Blend until puréed. Cook this mixture in the oil until the water has cooked off and the mixture is mostly dry, 2 to 3 minutes. Proceed with the recipe.

Lentil and Sausage Stew

I love many a lentil dish, but they can start to feel kind of . . . austere . . . on day three or four. So the answer to soup boredom is to fatten it up. In this case, with sausage. It makes the soup silkier, plus the seasonings from the sausage mean you don't need to add many yourself. And you end up with a bowl of stew you could eat for days.

SERVES 4

1 Tbsp extra-virgin olive oil, plus more for garnish

2 hot or sweet Italian sausages, fully thawed and casings removed

2 celery stalks, chopped

2 carrots, peeled and chopped

1 onion, any kind, peeled and chopped

2 garlic cloves, peeled and minced

1 tsp kosher salt

¼ tsp freshly ground black pepper

¼ cup [60 g] tomato paste

1 cup [200 g] brown or green lentils, rinsed

One 10 oz [280 g] bag frozen greens

½ cup [15 g] grated Parmesan cheese

In a large pot over medium-high heat, warm the oil until it shimmers. Add the sausage and quickly start breaking it up with a spoon into small pieces. Cook, stirring only occasionally, until the sausage is well browned and cooked through, 5 to 8 minutes. Use a slotted spoon to transfer the sausage to a bowl, leaving as much fat as possible in the pot.

Lower the heat to medium and add the celery, carrot, onion, and garlic, along with the salt and pepper (if you used sweet Italian sausage, you might want to add more pepper). Cook, stirring to scrape up the good stuff from the bottom of the pot, until the onion starts to turn golden, 8 to 10 minutes. Add the tomato paste and stir to coat the vegetables. Cook, stirring constantly, long enough to cook the tomato paste but before anything on the bottom of the pot burns, about 1 minute.

Add the lentils, the cooked sausage, and 6 cups [1.4 L] of water to the pot and bring to a boil. Lower the heat so the soup simmers steadily and cook, uncovered and stirring occasionally, until the lentils are tender,

25 to 30 minutes. Stir in the greens and continue cooking until the lentils are falling apart, another 10 to 15 minutes. Ladle the stew into bowls, garnish with a drizzle of olive oil and the cheese, and serve hot.

FRESHEN IT!

—

Most winter produce goes very well with sausage. Try adding chopped butternut squash with the lentils, or replacing the greens with a fresh, bitter variety like escarole.

Black Bean Burgers and Slaw

Veggie burgers are a great way to make beans interesting if you're feeling a little bean fatigue. They make humble ingredients seem so . . . special.

Buns are optional, but if you've got them, all the better.

SERVES 4

BURGERS

1 cup [60 g] panko bread crumbs

1 large egg

1 carrot, peeled and roughly chopped

½ onion, peeled and roughly chopped

1 garlic clove, peeled and roughly chopped

2 Tbsp soy sauce

1 Tbsp white or yellow miso

½ tsp kosher salt

½ tsp ground cumin

Two 14 oz [400 g] cans black beans, drained and rinsed

1 Tbsp vegetable oil

SLAW

2 Tbsp vegetable oil

2 Tbsp fresh lime juice

½ tsp kosher salt

½ tsp paprika, sweet or hot

4 cups [240 g] very thinly sliced cabbage

TO MAKE THE BURGERS: Preheat the oven to 400°F [200°C]. Add all of the burger ingredients except the beans and oil to a food processor and pulse until the ingredients are minced. Add the beans and pulse 3 or 4 times, so it is chunky but not yet a paste. Take a pinch of the mixture and press it together; if it stays together, it's done, and if it crumbles, pulse another 1 or 2 times. If the mixture still doesn't hold together, add 1 Tbsp of water. That should do the trick. (If you don't have a food processor, grate the carrot, onion, and garlic into a large bowl. Combine the remaining ingredients in the bowl and mash with a spoon. Repeat the process of testing and pinching some of the mix until it holds together.)

Smear a rimmed baking sheet with the oil. Shape the burger mixture into four equal-size balls, place them on the baking sheet, and gently press them into patties, smooshing any split edges back together. Brush the tops of the burgers with some of the oil from the baking sheet. Transfer the sheet to the oven and bake until the burgers are crisp and browned on the outside, 20 to 25 minutes.

cont.

pantry to plate

TO MAKE THE SLAW: In a large bowl, whisk together the oil, lime juice, salt, and paprika until combined. Add the cabbage and toss with your hands to combine, squeezing the cabbage to start to soften it. Let the slaw sit at room temperature while the burgers bake, or for up to 45 minutes.

To serve, divide the burgers among four plates and top with a generous amount of slaw. Serve warm.

FRESHEN IT!

—

Garnish the burgers with even more fresh vegetables. Top with sliced avocados and add ½ cup [20 g] of chopped fresh cilantro to the slaw.

Black Bean Tacos

These tacos are great for dinner, but where I think they truly shine is lunch: Pack all the components separately, assemble easily, and eat a meal that feels much more elaborate than it actually is.

SERVES 4

2 Tbsp vegetable oil

1 small or ½ large onion, any kind, peeled and chopped

2 garlic cloves, peeled and chopped

2 tsp kosher salt

1 Tbsp adobo sauce from canned chipotles, or more if you like spice

Three 14 oz [400 g] cans black beans, drained and rinsed

4 cups [240 g] very thinly sliced cabbage

3 limes, 1 cut into wedges

¼ tsp ground cumin

12 small tortillas

1 cup [120 g] crumbled queso fresco or feta cheese, for garnish

In a small pot over medium-high heat, warm the oil until it shimmers. Add the onion, garlic, and 1 tsp of the salt. Cook, stirring often and lowering the heat if the onion starts to burn, until the onion is soft and golden, 8 to 10 minutes. Add the adobo sauce and stir a few times to let it caramelize slightly, then add the beans and 1 cup [240 ml] of water. Bring the mixture to a boil, then lower the heat so it simmers steadily. Cook, stirring occasionally, while you prepare the other ingredients, or for up to 30 minutes. Taste and add more adobo sauce if you'd like the beans to be spicier.

In a large bowl, mix the cabbage with the juice of 1 lime, the cumin, and the remaining 1 tsp of salt. Toss with your hands and squeeze the cabbage to start to soften it. Taste, and if you'd like more lime, or if the first was dry, add the juice from another. (This can also be made up to 1 day in advance and refrigerated; let it come to room temperature before using.)

cont.

Turn a gas burner to medium heat, or warm a small skillet over medium heat on an electric stove. Cook the tortillas, one at a time, until they are just barely charred on one side, about 30 seconds. Use tongs to flip each tortilla over and char on the other side, then transfer each one to a plate and cover with a clean towel. Repeat with the remaining tortillas.

Use a wooden spoon to partially mash the beans—only about one-fourth of the pot—to thicken the mixture so they'll hold better in the tacos. To serve, fill each tortilla with a spoonful of beans in the center, top with some of the cabbage mixture, and garnish with the queso fresco.

FRESHEN IT!

I like to add ¼ cup [10 g] of chopped fresh cilantro to the cabbage mixture and garnish with 4 radishes, thinly sliced, along with the other components.

Basic Tofu Stir-Fry

Is it a cookbook cliché to think there are still people who don't like the texture of tofu? Well, if you or someone you're feeding is hesitant to have it so prominently featured in a dish, assure them that with some special attention and TLC, they'll be seeking out the tofu on their plate instead of pushing it to the side. (I promise the nice, crisp tofu is worth using two pans.) Serve this with a side of Plain White Rice (page 72) to round out the meal.

SERVES 4

One 14 oz [400 g] block firm tofu, drained (see page 120)

½ tsp kosher salt

¼ tsp freshly ground black pepper

4 Tbsp [60 ml] vegetable oil, plus more as needed

One 10 oz [280 g] bag frozen broccoli

1 small or ½ large onion, any kind, peeled, halved, and sliced

3 garlic cloves, peeled and sliced

One 2 in [5 cm] piece fresh ginger, peeled and chopped

3 Tbsp soy sauce

Juice of 1 lemon

Cut the tofu in half lengthwise, then slice each half perpendicularly to make ½ in [12 mm] thick slices. Spread the slices on paper towels or a clean dish towel and blot both sides dry. Season the tofu with the salt and pepper.

In a nonstick skillet over medium-high heat, warm 2 Tbsp of the oil until it shimmers. Add the tofu in a single layer, making sure each piece has some personal space (meaning they shouldn't all be touching; you may need to work in batches). Cook, undisturbed, until the tofu is golden and crisp, 4 to 5 minutes. Carefully flip the tofu (watch out for oil splatters) and cook the other side the same way. Transfer the tofu to a bowl and repeat with the remaining tofu, if necessary.

cont.

In a separate large skillet over high heat, warm the remaining 2 Tbsp of oil until it shimmers. Add the frozen broccoli and cook, stirring often, until it's bright green and beginning to brown in spots but is not yet mushy, 1 to 2 minutes. Transfer to the bowl with the tofu.

If your pan is looking dry, add another 1 Tbsp of oil to the skillet. Add the onion and cook, stirring a few times, until it is just softened, 2 to 3 minutes. Add the garlic and ginger and cook, stirring constantly, until the garlic smells toasted, about 1 minute. Return the tofu and broccoli to the skillet along with the soy sauce, lemon juice, and ¼ cup [60 ml] of water. Cook, stirring constantly, until everything is heated through and has absorbed most of the sauce, about 1 minute. Serve right away.

FRESHEN IT!

—

So many vegetables would be good in place of, or in addition to, the broccoli. Use up to 2 cups [about 280 g] of chopped snow peas, green beans, shiitake or cremini mushrooms, any type of bell pepper, or greens like bok choy or kale.

PREPARING TOFU

◇◇◇◇◇

For the recipes in this book that call for tofu—and for life, generally—you'll need to do a little tofu prep before you can use it. To drain any tofu that isn't silken: Wrap the tofu in paper towels or a clean dishcloth and place it in a colander with something flat-bottomed and heavy over it to press out extra water. A plate or bowl, with a can of something on top, works perfectly. Let it drain for as long as you can—either while you prep the rest of the ingredients or for up to 30 minutes. Then uncover it, give it a squeeze, and blot it dry. Now you're ready to go!

FRESHEN IT!

In place of the greens, add 2 zucchini, quartered lengthwise and chopped, halfway through cooking so they poach until just crisp-tender.

Tofu and Chickpea Curry

Simple, fast, and protein-packed, this curry is flavorful but with ingredients that have been streamlined down to a pretty bare-bones list—great when you don't feel like measuring much of anything. Serve with Plain White Rice (page 72) or rice noodles cooked according to the package directions.

SERVES 4

One 14 oz [400 g] block firm tofu, drained (see facing page)

3 Tbsp vegetable oil

½ large or 1 small onion, preferably yellow, peeled and chopped

3 garlic cloves, peeled and minced

One 2 in [5 cm] piece fresh ginger, peeled and minced

1 tsp kosher salt, plus more for seasoning

1 tsp ground turmeric

½ tsp coarsely ground black pepper, plus more for seasoning

One 14 oz [420 ml] can coconut milk

One 14 oz [400 g] can chickpeas, drained and rinsed

One 10 oz [280 g] package frozen greens

Cut the tofu into ½ in [12 mm] cubes. Spread the cubes on paper towels or a clean dish towel and blot dry.

In a large pot over medium-high heat, warm the oil until it shimmers. Add the onion, garlic, ginger, and salt to the pot. Cook, stirring often and lowering the heat if the onion starts to burn, until the onion is soft and golden, 8 to 10 minutes.

Add the turmeric and pepper and cook, stirring constantly, until they are toasted and fragrant, about 30 seconds. Pour in the coconut milk and ½ cup [120 ml] of water and scrape any flavorful browned bits from the bottom of the pot.

Add the tofu and the chickpeas and bring the mixture to a boil. Lower the heat so the mixture simmers gently and cook, stirring occasionally, until the tofu and chickpeas are tender and the curry has thickened, 15 to 20 minutes. Add the greens—still frozen is fine—and cook until warmed through, another 5 to 6 minutes. Taste the stew and add more salt or pepper, if you like, then serve hot.

Tofu Satay

Usually an appetizer, this restaurant favorite becomes dinner with a side of rice and vegetable of your choice. If you don't have wooden or metal skewers at home, you can bake the tofu on a baking sheet as individual pieces.

SERVES 4

12 wooden or metal skewers

Two 14 oz [400 g] blocks firm tofu, drained (see page 120)

1 tsp kosher salt

½ tsp freshly ground black pepper

¾ cup [180 ml] coconut milk

2 limes

½ to 1 tsp red pepper flakes, depending on your affinity for heat

3 garlic cloves, peeled

One 2 in [5 cm] piece fresh ginger, peeled

If using wooden skewers, soak them in water for 15 minutes. Cut the tofu in half lengthwise, then slice each half perpendicularly to make 1 in [2.5 cm] thick slices. Spread the slices on paper towels or a clean dish towel and blot both sides dry. Season the tofu with ½ tsp of the salt and the black pepper.

In a medium bowl, combine the coconut milk, juice from the limes, red pepper flakes, and remaining ½ tsp of salt. Use a Microplane or the smallest holes on a box grater to grate the garlic and ginger into the mixture. Stir to combine.

Dry the skewers (if you've been soaking them) and thread 4 pieces of tofu onto each skewer. Lay the skewers in a shallow baking dish and pour the marinade over the tofu. Rotate the skewers so every side is coated. At this point, you can cover them and marinate for up to 24 hours in the refrigerator.

Preheat the broiler and position the rack as close as possible to the heat source. Line a rimmed baking sheet with aluminum foil. When the broiler is hot, shake any excess marinade off the skewers and place them on the prepared sheet. Transfer the sheet to the oven and broil, watching like a hawk, until the tops are bubbly and browned, anywhere from

3 to 10 minutes, depending on your broiler. Flip the skewers and repeat on the other side. Remove the sheet from the oven, brush the tofu with more marinade, and repeat, cooking only for a minute or so on each side. Serve the tofu hot or at room temperature

FRESHEN IT!

—

Obviously, satay calls for a cucumber salad: Partially peel an 8 oz [230 g] cucumber (alternate between peeling a strip of skin off and leaving a strip of skin on), then halve the cucumber lengthwise and coarsely chop. Slice a quarter of a red onion very thinly. Mix the cucumbers and onion with 3 Tbsp of lime juice, 1 Tbsp of soy sauce, and a big pinch of salt. Let the salad marinate for a few minutes before serving.

Saag Tofu

Here's an easy and vegan version of the very popular Indian dish. Depending on how your pantry looks, this dish could end up several steps away from the inspiration—a coconut, kale, and tofu curry— but it still makes for a hearty meal served with Plain White Rice (page 72). If you like your dish a little saucier—this is pretty thick— you can add an additional half can of coconut milk (but I opted to not have half a can languishing in the refrigerator).

SERVES 4

One 14 oz [400 g] block firm or extra-firm tofu, drained (see page 120)

3 Tbsp vegetable oil

1 onion, preferably yellow, peeled and chopped

3 garlic cloves, peeled and minced

One 1 in [2.5 cm] piece fresh ginger, peeled and minced

1½ tsp kosher salt, plus more for seasoning

½ tsp freshly ground black pepper, plus more for seasoning

1 tsp ground turmeric

½ tsp ground cumin

¼ to ½ tsp red pepper flakes, depending on your affinity for heat

One 14 oz [420 ml] can coconut milk

1 lb [455 g] frozen spinach or kale, thawed

1 lemon or lime, cut into wedges, for serving

Cut the tofu into ½ in [12 mm] cubes. In a large skillet over medium-high heat, warm the oil until it shimmers, then add the onion, garlic, ginger, salt, and black pepper. Cook, stirring often and lowering the heat if the onion starts to burn, until the onion is soft and golden, 8 to 10 minutes. Add the turmeric, cumin, and red pepper flakes and cook until the spices are fragrant, about 30 seconds.

Add the coconut milk, spinach, and tofu and bring the mixture to a boil. Lower the heat so it simmers steadily and cook, stirring only occasionally, until the tofu has warmed through, 10 to 15 minutes. Taste and add more salt and pepper, if necessary. Serve hot with lemon or lime wedges.

FRESHEN IT!
—

Instead of the red pepper flakes, chop 1 fresh green chile (like a serrano or jalapeño), and garnish the final dish with ¼ cup [10 g] of chopped fresh cilantro.

pantry to plate

Kimchi Tofu Stew

Eating kimchi makes me feel like I'm doing something good for my body, so putting it into stew form feels like health, squared. This dish is highly recommended for days when you're sick, hung over, or just looking to have something that will make your insides feel loved.

SERVES 4

2 Tbsp vegetable oil

1 onion, preferably yellow, peeled and chopped

3 garlic cloves, peeled and minced

One 2 in [5 cm] piece fresh ginger, peeled and minced

½ tsp kosher salt

2 Tbsp soy sauce

2 large all-purpose potatoes like Yukon gold, coarsely chopped

1½ cups [225 g] chopped kimchi, or more if you like, plus a splash of the brine

One 14 oz [400 g] block tofu (ideally silken, but firm is fine), drained (see page 120)

¼ cup [60 g] white or yellow miso

In a large pot over medium-high heat, warm the oil until it shimmers. Add the onion, garlic, ginger, and salt. Cook, stirring often and lowering the heat if the onion starts to burn, until the onion is soft and golden, 8 to 10 minutes.

Pour in 6 cups [1.4 L] of water and the soy sauce and bring to a boil. Add the potatoes and cook, stirring occasionally, until the potatoes are just tender, 12 to 15 minutes. Add the kimchi and brine, then use your hands to break the tofu over the pot into spoon-able pieces and continue cooking until the tofu is warmed through, 3 to 5 minutes. Remove the pot from the heat. In a small bowl, whisk the miso with ¼ cup [60 ml] of warm water until smooth. Add the miso to the pot and stir to combine. Taste and add more kimchi, if you like. Serve hot.

FRESHEN IT!

Omit the onion and instead use the whites of 5 scallions, chopped. In place of the potatoes, peel and chop enough daikon radish to yield 2 cups [230 g]. Garnish with the chopped scallion greens.

pantry to plate

Eat Your *Veggies*

One of my goals with this book was to make sure the dishes would all feel balanced and healthy, and to me that means vegetables. Even when you're cooking from your pantry, it's very possible to make a meal centered around vegetables. Here are just ten ways to feature potatoes, broccoli, peas, cabbage, and more.

Cabbage Chopped Salad

Don't let the name fool you; this salad is something you'd want to make even if you weren't shopping your pantry. It's a perfect lunch or light dinner, though a side of some simple noodles or soup wouldn't be overkill.

SERVES 4

1 large onion, preferably red, peeled

2 limes

1½ tsp kosher salt, plus more for seasoning

6 Tbsp [90 ml] vegetable oil

3 Tbsp coconut milk

1 Tbsp white or yellow miso

One 1 in [2.5 cm] piece fresh ginger, peeled and minced

1 garlic clove, peeled and minced

One 14 oz [400 g] block extra-firm tofu, drained (see page 120)

Freshly ground black pepper

½ small head cabbage, any kind (about 1 lb [455 g])

3 carrots

First, pickle the onion: Halve it through the stem end and reserve half for another use (or make a double batch of pickled onions). Peel the remaining half and place it cut-side down on your cutting board. Slice the onion as thinly as you can (either direction is fine), then transfer it to a medium bowl and mix it with the juice of 1 of the limes and 1 tsp of the salt. Set aside to pickle while you prepare the rest of the ingredients.

In a small bowl, whisk together 3 Tbsp of the oil, the coconut milk, miso, ginger, garlic, and the juice of the remaining lime. Taste and add salt, if you like. Set aside or cover and refrigerate for up to 3 days.

Blot the tofu dry with paper towels or a clean dish towel, then cut it into ½ in [12 mm] cubes. In the largest nonstick skillet you have over medium-high heat, warm the remaining 3 Tbsp of oil until it shimmers. Add the tofu in a single layer, making sure

cont.

each piece has some personal space (meaning they shouldn't all be touching; you may need to work in batches). Cook, undisturbed, until the tofu is golden and crisp, 4 to 5 minutes. Flip the tofu and cook the other side the same way. Transfer the tofu to a paper towel–lined plate and repeat with the remaining tofu, if necessary. Season the tofu with the remaining ½ tsp of salt and pepper to taste.

Cut the core out of the cabbage, then cut the cabbage into several pieces of a manageable size. Using a mandoline (preferable) or a sharp knife (good alternative), slice the cabbage as thinly as you can manage. Transfer the cabbage to a large bowl (if your cabbage was particularly large, don't feel like you need to use the whole half). Use a vegetable peeler to peel the carrots, then continue peeling to make carrot ribbons, until you've shaved as much of the carrot as you can. Add the ribbons to the cabbage.

Drain the onions and add as many as you like to the cabbage along with the fried tofu. Pour about two-thirds of the dressing over everything and toss to combine. Taste, and add more dressing, if you like. Serve at room temperature.

FRESHEN IT!
—
Chop 3 scallions and 2 small cucumbers or half a large cucumber and add them to the salad.

Kimchi Potato Pancakes

Recently, when I was craving a kimchi pancake and was unwilling to leave home for the actual ingredients, I came up with this dish. You really can't go wrong with spicy fried potatoes. The kimchi means that these don't get quite as crisp as all-potato pancakes, but the combination of potatoes, onions, and pickled cabbage is intoxicating, so I don't really mind.

Serve these pancakes with a simple vegetable side like Beans and Greens (page 191) or an easy soup like Carrot Ginger Soup (page 48) to round out the meal.

SERVES 3 TO 4

1 cup [150 g] kimchi

2 lb [910 g] Yukon gold potatoes, peeled

1 small or ½ large onion, preferably yellow, peeled

2 large eggs, whisked

1 tsp kosher salt

½ tsp freshly ground black pepper

Vegetable oil, for frying

Squeeze as much liquid out of the kimchi as you can (you can reserve it for Kimchi Tofu Stew on page 126). Coarsely chop the kimchi and place it in a large bowl.

Using the largest holes on a box grater, grate the potatoes and the onion. Place the grated potatoes and onion in a colander and, taking a handful at a time, squeeze out the liquid, then squeeze some more—you'll be surprised how much there is. Place the squeezed potato-onion mixture into the bowl with the kimchi. Add the eggs, salt, and pepper and toss gently to combine.

Preheat the oven to 200°F [100°C]. In a large skillet over medium heat, warm 2 Tbsp of the oil until it

cont.

shimmers. Use a ¼ cup [60 ml] measure to portion out as many pancakes as will fit in the pan without touching each other after flattening them a bit with a fork. Cook the pancakes, undisturbed, until they are golden around the edges, 3 to 5 minutes. Flip and cook until the other side is golden and the pancakes are cooked through, another 2 to 3 minutes. Transfer the pancakes to a plate and keep them warm in the oven. Repeat with the remaining mixture, adding more oil as needed, and eat as soon as you have finished cooking.

FRESHEN IT!

Omit the onion and use 4 scallions, cut into 1 in [2.5 cm] pieces, and add 1 cup [85 g] of bean sprouts.

Spiced Peas

I had a version of this dish in the bookmarks folder for over a decade until recently (apparently). I can't find the original link anymore, but I make a version often enough that I don't need it. It's crazy easy, super delicious, and will make you feel like some kind of genius for stretching a bag of peas into dinner. Serve with Plain White Rice (page 72).

SERVES 4

2 Tbsp vegetable oil

1 small or ½ large onion, any kind, peeled and chopped

3 garlic cloves, peeled and minced

One 1 in [2.5 cm] piece fresh ginger, peeled and minced

1 tsp kosher salt, plus more for seasoning

½ tsp ground cumin

½ tsp freshly ground black pepper

¼ tsp ground turmeric

¼ to ½ tsp red pepper flakes, depending on your affinity for heat

¾ cup [180 ml] coconut milk

4 whole canned tomatoes, chopped

One 10 oz [280 g] bag frozen peas

In a large pot over medium-high heat, warm the oil until it shimmers. Add the onion, garlic, ginger, and salt. Cook, stirring often and lowering the heat if the onion starts to brown, until the onion is soft and golden, 8 to 10 minutes. Add the cumin, black pepper, turmeric, and red pepper flakes and cook, stirring constantly, until they smell fragrant, about 30 seconds.

Pour in the coconut milk and the chopped tomatoes and bring to a boil. Lower the heat so the mixture simmers steadily and cook, stirring occasionally, for 15 minutes (just to let the flavors come together). Add the peas and continue cooking, stirring every once in a while, until they are warmed through and the tomatoes have started to break down, another 5 to 8 minutes. Taste the sauce, add more salt, if you like, and serve hot.

FRESHEN IT!
—

Instead of canned tomatoes and red pepper flakes, use 4 small fresh tomatoes, chopped, and 1 small chile, minced and added with the onion. Cook for 20 minutes before adding the peas.

pantry to plate

Stewed Potatoes and Broccoli

For every three meals I'd never make again, scrounged together from an empty refrigerator, there are dishes like this one: a cross between a stewed potato dish from Madhur Jaffrey and aloo gobi, but subbing broccoli for cauliflower. It's miles ahead of soba noodles with pesto or a cabbage gratin made with milk instead of cream (do not try at home).

SERVES 4

3 Tbsp butter

1 onion, any kind, peeled and chopped

3 garlic cloves, peeled and minced

1½ tsp kosher salt, plus more for seasoning

1 cup [240 g] chopped canned tomatoes and juice

1 tsp ground turmeric

½ tsp freshly ground black pepper

1 lb [455 g] all-purpose or waxy potatoes, cut into 1 in [2.5 cm] cubes

One 10 oz [280 g] bag frozen broccoli, thawed

Greek yogurt, for serving

In a large pot over medium-high heat, warm the butter until it melts. Add the onion, garlic, and salt. Cook, stirring often and lowering the heat if the onion starts to brown, until the onion is soft and golden, 8 to 10 minutes. Mix in the tomatoes, turmeric, and pepper and cook for 1 to 2 minutes.

Add the potatoes and 1½ cups [360 ml] of water and bring the mixture to a boil. Lower the heat so the sauce simmers gently, cover, and cook until the potatoes are tender, 20 to 25 minutes.

When the potatoes are tender, remove the lid, mix in the broccoli, and cook until the sauce has thickened, 10 to 12 minutes. Taste and add more salt, if you like, and serve hot, with a dollop of yogurt on top.

FRESHEN IT!

Make it more like aloo gobi and use 1 head of cauliflower, chopped into 1 in [2.5 cm] pieces. Add it with the potatoes and up the water to 2 cups [480 ml].

Giant Stuffed Cabbage

This recipe takes a lot of liberties with this comfort food standard, but that just means less time assembling for you. Unfortunately, I can't make magic happen to get this on the table in less than 30 minutes, but I can promise that you're in for a treat.

SERVES 4

TOMATO SAUCE

One 28 oz [800 g] can tomatoes

½ large onion, any kind, peeled and coarsely chopped

2 garlic cloves, peeled and chopped

1 tsp kosher salt

1 tsp paprika, sweet or hot

½ tsp freshly ground black pepper

¼ tsp red pepper flakes

2 Tbsp extra-virgin olive oil

STUFFED CABBAGE

3 Tbsp extra-virgin olive oil

½ large onion, any kind, peeled and chopped

½ tsp kosher salt

1 cup [200 g] long-grain white rice, rinsed (see page 72)

cont.

TO MAKE THE TOMATO SAUCE: Combine all the ingredients except the oil in a blender or food processor and pulse 7 or 8 times to chop, but not purée, everything. In a large pot over medium heat, warm the oil until it shimmers. Pour the mixture into the pot and bring it to a boil. Lower the heat so it simmers gently, cover, and cook, stirring every so often, while you prepare the remaining ingredients, or for 20 to 30 minutes.

TO MAKE THE STUFFED CABBAGE: Preheat the oven to 350°F [180°C]. In a large skillet over medium-high heat, warm 2 Tbsp of the oil until it shimmers. Add the onion and salt. Cook, stirring often and lowering the heat if the onion starts to brown, until the onion is soft and golden, 8 to 10 minutes. Add the rice and lentils and cook, stirring often, until you can hear crackling. Remove from the heat and stir in the black pepper.

cont.

½ cup [100 g] brown or green lentils, rinsed

½ tsp freshly ground black pepper

1 large green cabbage

Greek yogurt, for serving

Peel off the large outer leaves of the cabbage, trying to keep them whole. Reserve any leaves that are a little more flexible and can lie (mostly) flat. Mix 1 cup [240 ml] of water into the warm tomato sauce.

Use the remaining 1 Tbsp of oil to coat a 9 in [23 cm] square baking pan. Spread 1 cup [240 ml] of the tomato sauce on the bottom of the pan. Line the bottom and sides of the pan with a layer of the outermost, toughest leaves, ripping them as necessary so they lie flat. Spread the rice and lentil mixture over the cabbage, then top with the reserved softer cabbage leaves, tucking some into the sides so it encases the filling. Pour 2 cups [480 ml] of the tomato sauce and ½ cup [60 ml] of water over the top, cover the pan tightly with foil, and transfer it to the oven. Bake for 1 hour, then check to make sure the rice and lentils are tender. If not, cook for another 15 minutes. Check again and continue baking until the rice is tender, no more than 80 to 95 minutes total. When the stuffed cabbage is ready, remove the pan from the oven and let sit for 10 minutes.

To serve, slice the cabbage and top with a dollop of yogurt.

FRESHEN IT!
—
Add ¼ cup [10 g] of chopped fresh dill and ½ cup [20 g] of chopped fresh parsley to the rice mixture before assembling the cabbage.

Veggie Tostadas with Spicy "Mayo"

This dish does have a lot of components, but the extra work makes everyday ingredients like beans and broccoli sing. You'll probably have some of the components left over—like the "mayo" or beans—but they can be the head start on whatever your next meal happens to be. That's never a bad thing.

SERVES 4

SPICY "MAYO"

4 oz [115 g] silken tofu (firm will work too, be sure to drain it—see page 120)

½ cup [120 ml] vegetable oil

2 Tbsp fresh lime juice

½ chipotle pepper in adobo sauce plus 1 tsp adobo sauce, plus more for seasoning

½ tsp kosher salt

VEGGIE TOSTADAS

1 large potato, any kind, cut into ½ in [12 mm] pieces

One 10 oz [280 g] bag frozen broccoli

5 Tbsp [75 ml] vegetable oil

1 tsp kosher salt

8 corn tortillas

2 garlic cloves, peeled and minced

cont.

Preheat the oven to 425°F [220°C].

TO MAKE THE SPICY "MAYO": Combine all the ingredients in a blender or food processor and purée until smooth. If you don't have a blender, add all of the ingredients except the oil to a food processor and turn on the machine. Slowly drizzle in the oil while the machine is running. If using firm tofu, you may have to add water, 1 tsp at a time, to get it to a drizzle-able consistency. Taste and add more chipotle, if you like. Cover and refrigerate until ready to serve, or for up to 3 days.

TO MAKE THE VEGGIE TOSTADAS: On a rimmed baking sheet, mix the potato and broccoli with 2 Tbsp of the oil and season with ½ tsp of the salt. Spread the vegetables in an even layer and transfer to the oven. Bake, undisturbed, for 15 minutes, then stir and continue roasting until the potatoes are golden and the broccoli is charred in spots, another 15 to 20 minutes.

cont.

½ tsp ground cumin

Two 14 oz [400 g] cans black beans, drained and rinsed

2 cups [120 g] very thinly sliced cabbage

1 cup [120 g] crumbled queso fresco or feta cheese

1 lime, cut into wedges

Meanwhile, brush the tortillas front and back with 1 Tbsp of the oil and place on another baking sheet, making sure the tortillas overlap as little as possible. Transfer to the oven and bake until the tortillas are crispy, 8 to 10 minutes.

In a small pot over medium heat, warm the remaining 2 Tbsp of oil until it shimmers. Add the garlic and cumin and cook, stirring constantly, until the garlic just starts to turn golden around the edges, 1 to 2 minutes. Add the beans and ½ cup [120 ml] of water and bring the mixture to a boil. Using the back of a wooden spoon, mash the beans until they are as creamy or chunky as you like them. Remove from the heat, add the remaining ½ tsp of salt, and keep warm.

To assemble the tostadas, spread each tortilla with some beans, top with a generous heap of roasted vegetables, about ¼ cup [15 g] of the cabbage, and garnish with the queso fresco. Drizzle some of the spicy mayo over the top of each tostada and serve with the lime wedges on the side.

FRESHEN IT!

—

Instead of the broccoli, add the kernels from 2 ears of fresh corn and 1 sliced bell pepper to the pan with the potato and expect the roasting time to increase by 10 to 15 minutes. Garnish with chopped fresh cilantro.

Roasted Vegetables with Tahini Sauce

Can a plate (or bowl—it's up to you) of roasted veggies be dinner?
Yes. Absolutely. With a mix of filling root vegetables and lighter
ones, you've got your whole bowl-for-dinner, minus the grains. But
if you are concerned about being satiated, you can cut a block of
tofu into 1 in [2.5 cm] cubes and add it to the pan before roasting.

SERVES 4

ROASTED VEGETABLES

2 large potatoes, cut into 1 in [2.5 cm] pieces

2 sweet potatoes, cut into 1 in [2.5 cm] pieces

4 Tbsp [60 ml] extra-virgin olive oil

1 tsp kosher salt, plus more for seasoning

1 tsp paprika, sweet or hot

1 large onion, any kind, peeled and cut into 1 in [2.5 cm] wedges

One 10 oz [280 g] bag frozen broccoli

½ small head cabbage, any kind, cut into 1 in [2.5 cm] wedges

½ tsp freshly ground black pepper

TO MAKE THE ROASTED VEGETABLES: Preheat the oven
to 425°F [220°C]. On a rimmed baking sheet, mix
together the chopped potatoes and sweet potatoes
and drizzle with 2 Tbsp of the oil. Season with ½ tsp
of the salt and the paprika. Toss everything together,
then spread the potatoes out in a single layer, making
sure each piece has some personal space (meaning
they shouldn't all be touching).

Place the onion, broccoli, and cabbage onto another
rimmed baking sheet, drizzle with the remaining
2 Tbsp of oil, the remaining ½ tsp of salt, and the
pepper. Gently toss the onions and broccoli to coat,
and carefully flip each cabbage wedge and rub it with
some oil and seasoning from the pan.

Place the baking sheets in the oven and bake for
15 minutes, undisturbed. Check both sheets, and
if you see any signs of burning, stir the veggies and
switch their positions. If the veggies haven't browned

TAHINI SAUCE

½ cup [110 g] tahini

½ tsp kosher salt, plus more for seasoning

1 garlic clove, peeled

1 lemon

at all, continue baking for another 5 minutes. When the vegetables are browned and crisp on the bottom, stir all the vegetables and carefully flip the cabbage wedges. Switch the pans' positions—whichever was on the higher rack goes to the lower rack and vice versa—and continue baking until everything is tender, another 15 to 20 minutes, depending on your oven.

TO MAKE THE TAHINI SAUCE: While the vegetables are roasting, bring a small pot of water to a boil. In a medium bowl, combine the tahini and salt. Use a Microplane to grate the garlic into the bowl, and grate about half the zest from the lemon (you can eyeball this). Halve the lemon and juice one half into the bowl. Start whisking and slowly add 1 cup [240 ml] of boiling water. The tahini will get very thick, then look chunky, then eventually thin out. Continue adding water until it is the consistency of melted chocolate, about ¾ cup [180 ml] of water total. Taste and add more salt or lemon juice, if you like.

To serve, divide the vegetables among four plates or serve family style, and pass the tahini sauce at the table for people to drizzle over their portions.

FRESHEN IT!
—

Place a handful of arugula or fresh spinach down on each plate before topping with the roasted vegetables.

Miso Potato Gratin

This gratin is inspired by a recipe I found in a Japanese cookbook for an eggplant gratin bound with a sauce made of tofu, heavy cream, and miso. *Ummmm*, delicious. Since heavy cream didn't make the list, I thin the tofu with water and add Parmesan to the sauce for good measure; it's just as good. Serve with something very green on the side to counteract all the potatoes and cheese.

SERVES 4

10 oz [280 g] tofu, preferably firm, drained (see page 120)

1 cup [30 g] grated Parmesan cheese

¼ cup [60 g] white or yellow miso

3 garlic cloves, peeled and chopped

1 tsp kosher salt

½ tsp freshly ground black pepper, plus more for seasoning

1 Tbsp butter

1½ lb [680 g] Yukon gold potatoes, peeled

Preheat the oven to 400°F [200°C]. In a blender or food processor, combine the tofu, ½ cup [15 g] of the cheese, the miso, garlic, salt, and pepper and add ½ cup [120 ml] of water. Blend until smooth. (If you don't have a blender or food processor, mash the ingredients with a fork and use a Microplane to grate the garlic.) Taste the sauce—it might be a bit salty, but remember that it will season the potatoes. If you'd like to add more pepper, do so now.

Use the butter to coat the inside of a 9 in [23 cm] square baking dish. Slice the potatoes ¼ in [6 mm] thick, then place them in the prepared baking dish in an even layer. Pour the miso sauce over the potatoes and spread evenly. Cover the dish with foil.

Bake the gratin for 45 minutes. Carefully remove the dish from the oven and check the potatoes; they should be tender when poked with a fork. If not, re-cover the pan and bake for another 10 minutes. When the potatoes are tender, remove and discard the foil, scatter the remaining ½ cup [15 g] of cheese on the top, and bake, uncovered, until the top is melted and browned in spots, another 12 to 15 minutes.

Let the gratin set for 10 minutes before slicing and serving.

FRESHEN IT!

This dish is *technically* made with all fresh vegetables, though I understand it might not seem like that. To give the dish a little hint of green, add 3 or 4 thyme sprigs on top of the potatoes for the first round of baking, then remove them before adding the cheese.

Baked Sweet Potatoes with Spicy Lentils

When I'm in a cooking rut, I tend to make the same thing with different ingredients: chop it all up, put it in a pot, and stew it. Sometimes, though, all it takes is reimagining how the ingredients might fit together to get out of said rut. Sweet potato and lentil stew is fine and filling. Crisp baked sweet potatoes with a spicy lentil "chili"? *Exciting.*

SERVES 4

3 Tbsp extra-virgin olive oil

4 sweet potatoes, halved lengthwise

1 tsp kosher salt

¼ tsp freshly ground black pepper

2 carrots, peeled and chopped

½ large onion, any kind, peeled and chopped

2 garlic cloves, peeled and minced

1 Tbsp tomato paste

½ tsp ground cumin

1½ cups [300 g] green or brown lentils, rinsed

1 chipotle pepper in adobo sauce

1 cup [240 g] Greek yogurt, for serving

Preheat the oven to 400°F [200°C]. Brush 1 Tbsp of the oil onto the cut sides of the potatoes and season with ¼ tsp of the salt and the pepper. Place the potatoes cut-side down on a baking sheet and transfer to the oven. Bake, mostly undisturbed but checking occasionally, until the potatoes are tender and the cut side is golden brown, 40 to 45 minutes.

Meanwhile, make the lentils. In a large pot over medium-high heat, warm the remaining 2 Tbsp of oil until it shimmers. Add the carrots, onion, garlic, and the remaining ¾ tsp of salt. Cook, stirring often and lowering the heat if the onion starts to burn, until the onion is soft and golden, 8 to 10 minutes. Add the tomato paste and cumin and cook, stirring constantly, long enough to cook the tomato paste but before anything on the bottom of the pot burns, about 1 minute.

cont.

Add the lentils, chipotle pepper (left whole), and 3 cups [720 ml] of water to the pot and bring to a boil. Lower the heat so the mixture simmers gently and cook, stirring occasionally and adding water a ¼ cup [60 ml] at a time if the pan dries out, until the lentils are very tender and the mixture is thick like chili, 30 to 35 minutes. Taste and mash the chipotle if you'd like it spicier, or remove and discard it.

To serve, place two potato halves, cut-side up, into a shallow bowl and spoon the lentil mixture over the top. Finish with a dollop of yogurt and serve hot.

FRESHEN IT!
—
Top each portion with diced fresh avocado and chopped raw onion for a loaded-baked-potato kind of vibe.

Baked Polenta with Greens and Tomato Sauce

By now, you've probably picked up on the fact that a simple tomato sauce can turn any carb into dinner. The trend continues with polenta—a dish I always tell myself I need to make more often whenever I eat it. This version features crispy edges, creamy texture, and lots of cheese. Oh, *and* greens. All the major food groups, really.

SERVES 6

POLENTA

3 Tbsp butter

1 cup [140 g] polenta (I use Bob's Red Mill, or look for fine-ground)

One 10 oz [280 g] bag frozen greens, thawed

½ cup [15 g] grated Parmesan cheese

1 tsp kosher salt

TOMATO SAUCE

2 Tbsp extra-virgin olive oil

3 garlic cloves, peeled and smashed

Pinch red pepper flakes

One 28 oz [800 g] can whole tomatoes

1½ tsp kosher salt

½ tsp freshly ground black pepper

TO MAKE THE POLENTA: Preheat the oven to 425°F [220°C]. Coat the inside of a 9 in [23 cm] square baking dish with 1 Tbsp of the butter. In a large pot, bring 4 cups [960 ml] of water to a boil. Start whisking and steadily pour in the polenta. Continue whisking until you've added all the polenta and there are no lumps, 1 to 2 minutes. Lower the heat so the polenta bubbles gently and cook, stirring every minute or so, for 15 minutes. Remove the pot from the heat and stir in the remaining 2 Tbsp of butter, the greens, ¼ cup [8 g] of the cheese, and the salt. Pour the mixture into the prepared baking dish and spread it into an even thickness.

Transfer the dish to the oven and bake until the edges are golden and the polenta feels firm in the center, 25 to 30 minutes.

cont.

TO MAKE THE TOMATO SAUCE: In a large pot over medium-high heat, warm the oil until it shimmers. Add the garlic and cook, stirring often, until it is golden and fragrant, about 1 minute. Add the red pepper flakes and stir once, then immediately pour in the tomatoes and their juices and break up the tomatoes with the back of your spoon. Bring the sauce to a boil and add the salt and pepper. Lower the heat so the sauce simmers steadily, cover, and cook until the polenta is ready, or for 15 to 20 minutes.

Remove the polenta from the oven and let it sit for 10 minutes. At the same time, uncover the sauce and let it cook, stirring occasionally, for 10 minutes. To serve, cut the polenta into squares, transfer to plates, and top with a spoonful of sauce. Garnish with the remaining cheese and eat hot.

FRESHEN IT!
—

Polenta and mushrooms are an ideal pairing. To make the sauce, add 8 oz [230 g] of cleaned and sliced cremini or other flavorful mushrooms to the pot with the garlic and season with ½ tsp of salt. Cover the pot and cook until the mushrooms have released all of their liquid, 5 to 7 minutes. Uncover and cook, undisturbed, until the pan is dry and the mushrooms are golden brown on one side, another 5 to 8 minutes. Continue with the recipe.

Protein
Heavy

Three delicious, versatile proteins—tuna, chicken thighs, and Italian sausage—will make your pantry meals feel decadent. But instead of using them just as flavoring, as we've been doing throughout the book, they're at the center of the plate (or bowl) in this chapter. I hope whatever you're craving can be found in these next pages.

Fancy Tuna Sandwich

There's a bakery close to my office that sells a delicious—if pricey—sandwich that inspired this one. But luckily, the ingredients all happen to be pantry staples. Its Mediterranean-with-Tunisian-vibes flavor makes it a dish you could even serve to guests (which you probably couldn't say about a regular tuna salad sandwich). Note: This is another opportunity for really good, crusty bread to soak up all the delicious flavors.

SERVES 4

½ large onion, preferably red, peeled

2 large eggs

3 Tbsp extra-virgin olive oil

1 Tbsp tomato paste

Juice of ½ lemon

¾ tsp kosher salt

¼ to ½ tsp red pepper flakes, depending on your affinity for heat

¼ tsp ground cumin

Two 6 oz [170 g] cans tuna, preferably packed in olive oil

8 slices crusty bread

1 large carrot, peeled and shredded

½ cup [70 g] roughly chopped pitted olives, preferably Kalamata

Place the onion cut-side down on your cutting board. Slice the onion as thinly as you can (either direction is fine), then transfer the slices to a medium bowl and cover with cold water. Set aside while you prepare the rest of the ingredients.

Fill a small pot with water and bring to a boil over medium-high heat. Using tongs or a large spoon, lower the eggs carefully and slowly into the water, one at a time (this helps prevent temperature shock and cracking). Cook the eggs for 8 minutes, then pour out the boiling water and fill the pot with cold water and ice. Let the eggs cool, then peel and thinly slice.

In a medium bowl, combine 1 Tbsp of the oil, the tomato paste, the lemon juice, salt, red pepper flakes, and cumin. Slowly pour in 1 Tbsp of hot water and whisk to combine. Add the tuna—including the oil—to the bowl and stir with a fork to combine and break up the tuna.

cont.

Preheat the broiler. Place the bread slices on a rimmed baking sheet and brush both sides with the remaining 2 Tbsp of oil. Transfer the pan to the oven and broil, watching like a hawk, until the bread is as toasted as you like. Turn over the slices and repeat on the other side.

To assemble the sandwiches, divide the tuna mixture among four pieces of toast and top with a few slices of egg. Drain the onions and pat dry with a paper towel. Pile on the onions, shredded carrot, and olives, then top with another slice of bread and press down. Serve right away, with lots of napkins.

FRESHEN IT!

Line the bottom piece of bread with fresh basil leaves before adding the tuna.

Tuna Patties

Canned fish gets the crab cake treatment. You could eat the main components as is, but with just a little bit of effort, your meal will feel infinitely more special. I prefer to eat these bun-less, but if you already have buns, that certainly gets you closer to a whole meal.

SERVES 4

½ cup [30 g] panko bread crumbs

Two 6 oz [170 g] cans tuna, preferably packed in olive oil

1 celery stalk, minced

¼ onion, preferably red, peeled and minced

¼ cup [35 g] chopped pitted olives

1 tsp kosher salt

½ tsp freshly ground black pepper

1 large egg

2 Tbsp extra-virgin olive oil

1 lemon, cut into wedges, for serving

In a large bowl, combine the bread crumbs, tuna and any oil, celery, onion, olives, salt, and pepper. Mix thoroughly, breaking up the tuna and evenly distributing the seasonings. Add the egg to the bowl and mix well.

Shape the mixture into four equal balls, place them on a plate, and gently press them into patties, smooshing any split edges back together. Transfer to the freezer for 20 to 30 minutes to chill (this is a great time to make side dishes).

In a large nonstick skillet over medium heat, warm the oil until it shimmers. Carefully place the patties in the skillet and cook, undisturbed, until the bottoms are golden brown, 4 to 5 minutes. Flip and repeat on the other side. Transfer the finished patties to plates and serve hot with a lemon wedge on the side.

FRESHEN IT!

Add ½ cup [20 g] of finely chopped fresh parsley to the tuna mixture before adding the egg.

Chipotle Chicken Tacos

This sauce is one of the reasons chipotles make it onto my list of pantry must-haves—they provide so much flavor, and fast. (Also because tacos are the perfect meal.)

You can mince the other half of the onion and use it as a garnish for the tacos, if you're into that kind of thing.

SERVES 4

4 bone-in, skin-on chicken thighs, fully thawed and patted dry

1 tsp kosher salt, plus more for seasoning

¼ tsp freshly ground black pepper

½ onion, any kind, peeled and chopped

3 garlic cloves, peeled and smashed

One 14 oz [400 g] can whole tomatoes

1 or 2 chipotle peppers in adobo sauce, depending on your affinity for heat

2 limes, 1 cut into wedges

12 small corn tortillas

2 cups [120 g] very thinly sliced green cabbage

Place the chicken thighs skin-side up on a cutting board or plate and season with the salt and black pepper. Heat a large pot over medium-high heat and add the chicken, skin-side down. Cook, undisturbed, until the skin is golden brown and doesn't stick to the pot, 8 to 10 minutes. Flip the chicken and cook on the other side until golden and crisp, 3 to 5 minutes. Transfer the chicken to a plate (it doesn't have to be fully cooked at this point). Pour off some of the fat, if you like.

Add the onion and garlic to the pot and cook, stirring to scrape up the good stuff from the bottom of the pot, until the onion starts to turn golden, 8 to 10 minutes. Add the tomatoes and chipotle and smash them with your spoon. Return the chicken thighs to the pot and try to submerge them as well as you can in the sauce. Cover the pot, turn the heat to medium, and cook until the chicken is tender and cooked through, 20 to 25 minutes.

When the chicken is ready, remove it from the pot and set aside for a few minutes to cool while you finish the sauce. Add the juice of 1 of the limes to the sauce. Using a handheld blender or a wooden spoon and some elbow grease, blend or mash the sauce into a smoother consistency—you don't need it completely smooth, but you want to break up some of the vegetables. Taste and add more salt or a little adobo sauce, if you like.

Remove the chicken skin and bones and discard, then use two forks to shred the chicken meat. Transfer the meat to a bowl and pour over 1 cup [240 ml] of the sauce and toss to coat. Cover and keep warm.

Turn a gas burner to medium, or heat a small skillet over medium heat on an electric stove. Cook the tortillas, one at a time, until they are just barely charred on one side, about 30 seconds. Use tongs to flip each tortilla over and char on the other side, then transfer each one to a plate and cover with a clean towel. Repeat with the remaining tortillas.

Fill each tortilla with a spoonful of the chicken, a large pinch of the cabbage, and a squeeze of lime, and serve warm.

FRESHEN IT!

Go crazy with the garnishes: Add sliced avocado, shaved radishes, or cilantro sprigs (or all three).

Sheet Pan Chicken Dinner

Miso butter, crisp chicken skin, potatoes, and carrots make for one mouthwatering meal ready in less than an hour—and tastes like it took all day.

SERVES 4

⅓ cup [80 g] white or yellow miso

4 Tbsp [55 g] butter, melted

1 tsp freshly ground black pepper

8 oz [230 g] potatoes, any kind, cut into 1 in [2.5 cm] chunks

4 carrots, peeled and cut into 1 in [2.5 cm] chunks

1 large onion, preferably red, peeled and cut into 1 in [2.5 cm] wedges

2 Tbsp vegetable oil

1 tsp kosher salt

8 bone-in, skin-on chicken thighs, fully thawed and patted dry

Preheat the oven to 425°F [220°C]. In a small bowl, mix together the miso, melted butter, and pepper thoroughly.

Place the potatoes, carrots, and onion on a rimmed baking sheet, drizzle them with the oil, then season with the salt. Toss everything to combine, then spread the vegetables evenly on the baking sheet. Nestle the chicken thighs into the vegetables, skin-side up, then generously drizzle the miso butter over the chicken. Pour any leftover butter on the vegetables.

Transfer the pan to the oven and bake until the chicken skin is a deep golden color and the chicken is cooked through, 45 to 55 minutes. To serve, transfer the chicken to a platter and the vegetables to a bowl, then pour any pan juices over each. Serve warm.

FRESHEN IT!

In place of the carrots and onions, use 1 pint [440 g] of whole cherry tomatoes and 1 bunch of whole scallions.

pantry to plate

Chicken Tagine

While *tagine* is a name for both the dish and the cooking vessel it's made in, this Moroccan stew can easily be made in any pot you've got—in this case, a wide skillet.

For the olives, I'm of the belief that people can handle olives with pits in their food as long as they have some warning, but if you disagree (or you're serving children), you can smash the olives with the side of your knife and remove the pits before adding them to the pan.

SERVES 4

8 bone-in, skin-on chicken thighs, fully thawed and patted dry

1½ tsp kosher salt

½ tsp freshly ground black pepper

1 onion, any kind, peeled, halved, and sliced

4 garlic cloves, peeled and sliced

1 Tbsp paprika, sweet or hot

1 tsp ground cumin

½ tsp ground turmeric

One 14 oz [400 g] can whole tomatoes

One 14 oz [400 g] can chickpeas, drained and rinsed

1 cup [160 g] whole olives, preferably green

1 lemon

Place the chicken thighs skin-side up on a cutting board or plate and season with 1 tsp of the salt and the pepper. Heat a large skillet over medium-high heat. Add the chicken, skin-side down, and cook, undisturbed, until the skin is golden brown and doesn't stick to the skillet, 8 to 10 minutes. Flip the chicken and cook on the other side until golden and crisp, 3 to 5 minutes. Transfer the chicken to a plate (it doesn't have to be fully cooked at this point).

Add the onion and garlic to the skillet and cook, stirring to scrape up the good stuff from the bottom of the skillet, until the onion starts to turn golden, 8 to 10 minutes. Add the paprika, cumin, and turmeric and cook until fragrant, less than 30 seconds.

Pour in the tomatoes and their juices, the chickpeas, olives, and the remaining ½ tsp of salt, then nestle the chicken into the sauce, skin-side up. Bring the mixture to a boil, then lower the heat so it simmers gently. Cover the skillet and cook, stirring if the sauce starts to scorch, until the chicken is tender and cooked through, 20 to 25 minutes.

When the chicken is ready, uncover the skillet and use your spoon to break up the tomatoes. If you like your chickpeas a little softer, remove the chicken and cook the stew for another 10 minutes. Squeeze the lemon over everything and serve hot.

FRESHEN IT!

Treat herbs like a vegetable and add them to the pot with the olives and tomatoes: Use ½ cup [20 g] (or more!) of chopped fresh parsley and the same amount of chopped fresh cilantro.

Coconut-Braised Chicken

Sounds so fancy, right? It is! But through the miracle of pantry ingredients and time, you too can have a mouthwateringly delicious dinner on a weeknight. (Or a weekend . . . I can't tell you when to cook these dishes.) Make sure you have a side on hand to make the most of the coconut sauce, like Plain White Rice (page 72) or rice noodles.

SERVES 4

8 bone-in, skin-on chicken thighs, fully thawed and patted dry

2 tsp kosher salt

½ tsp freshly ground black pepper

½ large or 1 small onion, any kind, peeled, halved, and sliced

3 garlic cloves, peeled and sliced

One 2 in [5 cm] piece fresh ginger, peeled and chopped

½ tsp ground turmeric

One 14 oz [420 ml] can coconut milk

2 limes, 1 cut into wedges for serving

Place the chicken thighs skin-side up on a cutting board or plate and season with 1 tsp of the salt and the pepper. Heat a large skillet over medium-high heat. Add the chicken, skin-side down, and cook, undisturbed, until the skin is golden brown and doesn't stick to the skillet, 8 to 10 minutes. Flip the chicken and cook on the other side until golden and crisp, 3 to 5 minutes. Transfer the chicken to a plate (it doesn't have to be fully cooked at this point).

Add the onion, garlic, ginger, and remaining 1 tsp of salt to the skillet and cook, stirring to scrape up the good stuff from the bottom of the skillet, until the onion starts to turn golden, 8 to 10 minutes. Add the turmeric and cook until fragrant, less than 30 seconds.

Pour in the coconut milk and nestle the chicken into the sauce, skin-side up. Bring the mixture to a boil, then lower the heat so it simmers gently. Cover the skillet and cook, basting the chicken occasionally, until the chicken is tender and cooked through, 20 to 25 minutes.

When the chicken is ready, uncover the skillet and add the zest and juice of 1 lime. Serve hot, with lime wedges on the side.

FRESHEN IT!

Add 2 medium eggplants, cut into large chunks and seasoned with 1 tsp of salt, to the pot after the chicken is removed and before the onion and aromatics go in. Cook until browned in spots, then transfer to the plate with the chicken. You may need to add 1 Tbsp of vegetable oil to the pot before adding the onion. Proceed with the recipe, returning the eggplant to the sauce with the chicken.

Greek Chicken

In the world of cuisine flavor profiles, I'm somewhat surprised I don't cook more Greek food. The cuisine utilizes most of my favorite ingredients—olives, feta cheese, tons of herbs—and fresh produce galore. Whenever someone talks about the Mediterranean diet, my mind immediately goes to Greece, and being in a beautiful mountainside town with whitewashed houses. . . . Where was I? Oh, right—serve this dish with crusty bread for soaking up every last bit of the sauce.

SERVES 4

8 bone-in, skin-on chicken thighs, fully thawed and patted dry

2 tsp kosher salt

½ tsp freshly ground black pepper

1 large onion, preferably red, peeled and chopped

4 garlic cloves, peeled and minced

¼ cup [60 ml] fresh lemon juice, plus 1 lemon, cut into wedges for serving

One 28 oz [800 g] can whole tomatoes

1 cup [160 g] whole olives, preferably Kalamata

½ cup [60 g] crumbled feta cheese

Preheat the oven to 425°F [220°C]. Place the chicken thighs skin-side up on a cutting board or plate and season with 1 tsp of the salt and the pepper. Warm a large ovenproof skillet over medium-high heat. Add the chicken, skin-side down, and cook, undisturbed, until the skin is golden brown and doesn't stick to the skillet, 8 to 10 minutes. Flip the chicken and cook on the other side until golden and crisp, 3 to 5 minutes. Transfer the chicken to a plate (it doesn't have to be fully cooked at this point).

Add the onion, garlic, and remaining 1 tsp of salt to the skillet and cook, stirring to scrape up the good stuff from the bottom of the skillet, until the onion starts to turn golden, 8 to 10 minutes. Add the lemon juice and cook, stirring constantly, until it reduces by about half, less than 1 minute.

Add the tomatoes and their juices, breaking up the tomatoes a bit with your spoon, then add the olives.

cont.

Nestle the chicken into the sauce, skin-side up. Bring the mixture to a boil, then carefully transfer the skillet—uncovered—to the oven. Cook, stirring occasionally, until the chicken is a deep golden color and cooked through, 20 to 25 minutes.

Remove the skillet from the oven, garnish with the feta, and serve hot, family style, passing the lemon wedges at the table.

FRESHEN IT!

Sorry to sound like a broken record about herbs—but they make every pantry meal so much better. Add 2 sprigs of fresh oregano (or 1 Tbsp dried) to the sauce before putting the skillet in the oven, and finish with lots of chopped fresh parsley.

Chicken Parm-esque

You can actually make something pretty close to the original dish without having to deal with breading and frying, which might even make this a *better* version than the original. Here, chicken is roasted with the tomato sauce (to take advantage of all the good chicken flavor), then topped with a generous amount of garlicky bread crumbs and Parmesan cheese.

SERVES 4

One 28 oz [800 g] can whole tomatoes

½ onion, any kind, peeled and coarsely chopped

2 tsp kosher salt

¼ tsp red pepper flakes

8 bone-in, skin-on chicken thighs, fully thawed and patted dry

½ tsp freshly ground black pepper

5 Tbsp [75 ml] extra-virgin olive oil

1 cup [60 g] panko bread crumbs

2 garlic cloves, peeled

½ cup [15 g] grated Parmesan cheese, or more if you love cheese

Preheat the oven to 425°F [220°C]. Place the tomatoes and their juices, onion, 1 tsp of the salt, and the red pepper flakes in a blender or food processor and pulse a few times until the mixture is mostly smooth. (If you don't have either appliance, omit the onion and break the tomatoes apart with your hands.) Pour the sauce into a large ovenproof skillet.

Place the chicken thighs skin-side up on a cutting board or plate and season all over with the remaining 1 tsp of salt and the black pepper. Transfer the chicken to the baking dish, nestling it in the sauce, skin-side up, and leaving as much of the skin exposed as possible. Drizzle the chicken with 1 Tbsp of the oil to help the skin crisp. Place the dish in the oven, uncovered, and bake until the chicken is cooked

cont.

through and the skin is golden, 35 to 40 minutes. If the chicken is cooked but the skin hasn't colored much, place under the broiler for 1 to 2 minutes to help it along.

In a large skillet over medium heat, warm the remaining 4 Tbsp [60 ml] of olive oil until it shimmers. Add the bread crumbs to the skillet and cook, stirring often, until they are golden and crisp, 8 to 10 minutes. Immediately transfer the bread crumbs to a heatproof bowl and use a Microplane to grate the garlic over the top, then stir.

When the chicken is done, transfer it to a serving platter. Stir the tomato sauce a few times, then spoon it over the chicken. Top with the garlicky bread crumbs and cheese, and serve hot. (If you aren't serving right away, keep the bread crumbs and Parmesan separate until just before serving.)

FRESHEN IT!
—

Sadly, fresh mozzarella is not a vegetable, but basil sure is! Add 1 large sprig of basil (or 2 small sprigs) to the baking dish with the sauce, and discard before serving. Top with torn fresh basil too, if you like.

Crispy Chicken Thighs

I originally called this recipe Oven-Fried Chicken, but I don't want you to get the wrong idea about a dish that's delicious in its own right. Oven-baked, breaded chicken is its own wonderful category, and this version has a bit of a kick from paprika and plenty of crunch from panko bread crumbs.

SERVES 4

2 eggs

1 cup [240 g] Greek yogurt

2 tsp kosher salt

½ tsp paprika, sweet or hot

½ tsp freshly ground black pepper

3 cups [180 g] panko bread crumbs

8 bone-in, skin-on chicken thighs, fully thawed and patted dry

1 Tbsp vegetable oil

Preheat the oven to 400°F [200°C]. In a large bowl, mix together the eggs, yogurt, 1 tsp of the salt, the paprika, and pepper. Pour the bread crumbs on a wide, flat plate. Season the chicken all over with the remaining 1 tsp of salt. Add the chicken to the bowl with the yogurt mixture and toss to coat. (At this point you can cover the bowl and refrigerate for up to 8 hours.) Grease a baking sheet with the oil.

Remove the chicken, one piece at a time, and place it in the bread crumbs. Press the bread crumbs onto the chicken so every bit of chicken is covered. Transfer the chicken to the prepared baking sheet and repeat with the remaining chicken, then transfer the sheet to the oven. Bake until the outside is golden and the chicken is cooked through (you can check by cutting a piece close to the bone and seeing if there is still pink inside), 40 to 45 minutes. Serve warm or at room temperature.

FRESHEN IT!
—
You're definitely going to need some vegetables on the side, but you could also garnish the finished chicken with about 2 Tbsp of chopped fresh chives.

Lentils in the Style of Cassoulet

This is French comfort food, pantry style, and is also made *way* lighter with only one type of meat (that's a good thing).

SERVES 6

5 Tbsp [75 ml] extra-virgin olive oil

6 Italian sausages, sweet or hot, fully thawed

2 celery stalks, chopped

1 onion, any kind, peeled and chopped

2 garlic cloves, peeled and minced

1 carrot, peeled and chopped

2¼ tsp kosher salt

½ tsp freshly ground black pepper

2 Tbsp tomato paste

½ tsp paprika

1½ cups [300 g] green or brown lentils, rinsed

1 cup [240 g] chopped canned tomatoes, with their juices

1 cup [60 g] panko bread crumbs

Preheat the oven to 375°F [190°C] and set the oven rack in the middle position. In a large ovenproof pot over medium-high heat, warm 1 Tbsp of the oil until it shimmers. Add the sausages and cook, undisturbed, until they are well browned on one side, 6 to 8 minutes. Turn the sausages and repeat on the another side, then transfer them to a plate (they don't need to be fully cooked at this point).

Add the celery, onion, garlic, carrot, 1 tsp of the salt, and the pepper to the pot and cook, stirring to scrape up the good stuff from the bottom of the pot, until the onion starts to turn golden, 8 to 10 minutes. Add the tomato paste and paprika and cook, stirring constantly, long enough to cook the tomato paste but before anything on the bottom of the pot burns, about 1 minute.

cont.

Add the lentils, tomatoes, and 1 tsp of the salt and stir to coat. Pour in 4½ cups [1 L] of water and bring everything to a boil. Carefully—very carefully—transfer the pot, uncovered, to the oven. Bake for 40 minutes.

While the lentils are baking, in a large skillet over medium heat, warm the remaining 4 Tbsp [60 ml] of olive oil until it shimmers. Add the bread crumbs to the pan and cook, stirring often, until they are golden and crisp, 8 to 10 minutes. Immediately transfer the bread crumbs to a heatproof bowl and season with the remaining ¼ tsp of salt.

After 40 minutes, remove the pot from the oven—again, carefully—stir the lentils, then top with the sausage and return the pot to the oven. Bake until the sausage is cooked through and the lentils are tender, another 25 to 35 minutes. When the lentils are done, sprinkle the bread crumbs over the top and bake for another 5 minutes. Serve hot.

FRESHEN IT!
—
Instead of canned tomatoes, use 1 large, fresh tomato, chopped, plus any of the juices.

Sausages Over Polenta

This dish is hearty, warming, and perfect for eight to nine months out of the year. (If you have a grill and want to grill the sausages, I'd say that bumps it up to twelve months a year.)

SERVES 4

1 cup [140 g] polenta (I use Bob's Red Mill, or look for fine-ground)

1½ tsp kosher salt

4 Italian sausages, sweet or hot, fully thawed

1 large onion, any kind, peeled, halved, and sliced

2 Tbsp butter

½ cup [15 g] freshly grated Parmesan cheese

In a large pot, bring 6 cups [1.4 L] of water to a boil. Start whisking and steadily pour in the polenta. Continue whisking until you've added all the polenta and there aren't any lumps, 1 to 2 minutes. Add 1 tsp of the salt, lower the heat so the polenta bubbles gently, and cook, stirring every minute or so and adding a splash of water if it's too thick for your liking, while you prepare the rest of the ingredients, 30 to 45 minutes total.

Meanwhile, warm a large skillet over medium-high heat. When the skillet is hot, add the sausage and cook, undisturbed, until the sausage is well browned, 6 to 8 minutes. Flip the sausage and cook until the other side is browned and the sausage is cooked through, another 6 to 8 minutes. Transfer the sausage to a plate. Add the onions to the skillet, stirring to scrape up the good stuff from the bottom of the pan, until they are soft and golden, another 8 to 10 minutes. Season the onions with the remaining ½ tsp of salt.

When the polenta is ready, remove the pot from the heat and stir in the butter and cheese. To serve, pour the polenta onto a serving platter or individual plates, top with the sausages, and spoon over the onions and any accumulated juices. Serve hot.

FRESHEN IT!

After you remove the sausage from the skillet, add 1 bunch of chopped fresh greens like chard or spinach and cook just until wilted, 1 to 2 minutes.

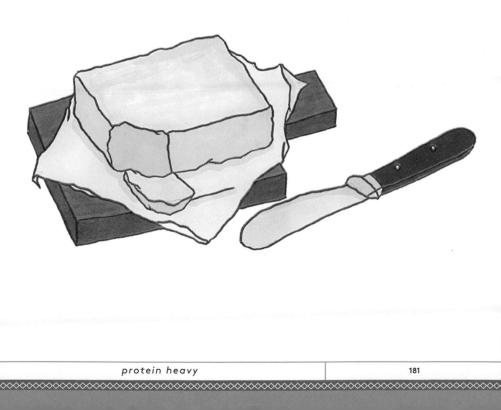

Sides (and Turning Them into Meals)

Many of the recipes in this book could use a helping hand in the form of added vegetables or protein to bump them up to a meal that feels special. But I know I certainly don't always feel like making more than one dish on weeknights, so I've also included strategies to turn these recipes into composed dishes if you're really craving, say, a crunchy salad or potatoes.

The Best Celery Salad

Celery salad almost feels like cheating—you can make a whole fresh, crunchy salad with the leftovers of something you probably bought for another recipe and had no idea what to do with (besides using it as a vehicle for peanut butter). It feels like it's basically free. Here's an Italian take on the perfect pantry side that's also pretty good on day two.

SERVES 4

½ garlic clove, peeled

3 Tbsp fresh lemon juice

1 tsp grated lemon zest

½ tsp kosher salt

Freshly ground black pepper

⅓ cup [80 ml] extra-virgin olive oil

4 cups [450 g] thinly sliced celery

Celery leaves (as many as possible)

⅓ cup [10 g] grated Parmesan cheese, using the largest holes on a box grater

Using a Microplane, grate the garlic into a small 8 oz [240 ml] jar and add the lemon juice, lemon zest, salt, and a few grinds of pepper. Close the jar and shake it a few times to combine, then add the oil and shake vigorously.

Place the celery, celery leaves, and cheese into a bowl and drizzle half the dressing over the top. Toss to combine, taste, and add more dressing, if you like. Serve at room temperature.

MAKE IT A MEAL

Make a batch of Plain White Rice (page 72) following the instructions to spread the cooked rice on a baking sheet to cool to room temperature. Instead of the amounts listed above, use 1 peeled garlic clove, ⅓ cup [80 ml] of lemon juice, 1 tsp of salt, and ⅔ cup [160 ml] of extra-virgin olive oil to make the dressing—you can keep the lemon zest at 1 tsp.

In the second step of the above recipe, when combining the celery, cheese, and dressing, add two 6 oz [170 g] cans of oil-packed tuna and half of the cooled rice and toss to combine.

pantry to plate

Chickpea Salad

Here's a great way to balance out carb-heavy mains (ahem, pasta). I like to cook canned chickpeas a little longer to soften them up, but if you're absolutely crunched for time, it's a step that can be skipped.

SERVES 4

Two 14 oz [400 g] cans chickpeas, drained and rinsed

2 tsp kosher salt

½ garlic clove, peeled

¼ cup [60 ml] extra-virgin olive oil

Juice of 1 lemon

¼ tsp paprika, sweet or hot

Pinch ground cumin

Freshly ground black pepper

1 large carrot, peeled and grated on the large holes of a box grater

¼ cup [35 g] chopped pitted olives

In a medium pot, cover the chickpeas with at least 2 in [5 cm] of water and bring to a boil. Add 1 tsp of the salt and cook for 10 minutes. Drain the chickpeas and set aside.

While the chickpeas are cooking, use a Microplane to grate the garlic into a large bowl. Add the oil, lemon juice, remaining 1 tsp of salt, paprika, cumin, and a few grinds of pepper and whisk to combine. Add the carrot to the dressing, then add the chickpeas and the olives. Toss to coat everything with the dressing and serve warm or at room temperature.

MAKE IT A MEAL
—
Double the carrots and olives and serve over Plain White Rice (page 72).

Coconut Rice

I think of this as "special occasion" rice since it adds a rich creaminess to any meal.

SERVES 4

1½ cups [300 g] long-grain white rice

One 14 oz [420 ml] can coconut milk

1 tsp kosher salt

MAKE IT A MEAL
—

While the rice cooks, make an easy sheet pan dinner with one 14 oz [400 g] block of tofu, drained (see page 120), cut into 1 in [2.5 cm] cubes; 1 large onion, cut into 1 in [2.5 cm] wedges; 1 sweet potato, cut into 1 in [2.5 cm] cubes; and one 10 oz [280 g] bag of frozen broccoli. Combine all of the ingredients on a rimmed baking sheet, drizzle with 3 Tbsp of vegetable oil, and sprinkle with 1 tsp of salt. Toss everything to coat. Place the sheet in an oven preheated to 425°F [220°C] and roast until everything is tender and browned, 40 to 50 minutes. Serve the rice topped with the vegetables and tofu with lime wedges on the side.

In a small pot with a tight-fitting lid, cover the rice with water and swirl it with your hands until the water is cloudy, taking care not to break any of the grains. Drain the rice into a colander and repeat until the water is clear. Shake off as much water as you can from the rice and transfer it back to the pot. Wrap the lid with a dish towel and securely knot the towel on top of the lid so the corners won't reach down into your stove's flame.

Add the coconut milk and 1½ cups [360 ml] of water to the pot along with the salt and bring to a boil over medium-high heat. Lower the heat so the water simmers gently and cook, undisturbed, until the surface of the rice looks dry and holes appear, 5 to 8 minutes. Turn the heat to very low, place the cloth-wrapped lid on the pot, and cook for 10 minutes. Remove from the heat and let sit, covered and undisturbed, for 10 minutes.

Use a fork to separate the grains (this is what "fluffing" means) and serve hot.

Potatoes with Lemon and Pepper

A bright, light potato salad with a simple lemon dressing that goes with just about everything.

SERVES 4

1 Tbsp plus 1½ tsp kosher salt

1½ lb [680 g] waxy potatoes, like new potatoes, cut into 1 in [2.5 cm] chunks

¼ cup [55 g] butter

Zest and juice of 1 lemon

1 tsp freshly ground black pepper

In a large pot, bring at least 8 cups [2 L] of water to a boil, then add 1 Tbsp of the salt. Add the potatoes and cook, stirring occasionally, until the pieces fall off a knife easily when pierced, 15 to 20 minutes. Drain the potatoes and immediately transfer to a large bowl.

Add the butter, lemon zest, lemon juice, pepper, and the remaining 1½ tsp of salt to the bowl and toss everything to combine and melt the butter. Serve hot or warm.

MAKE IT A MEAL

Make a fun spread inspired by Nicoise: Place the potatoes on a large serving platter (or individual plates) with one 10 oz [280 g] bag of steamed broccoli (this isn't traditional but you need some green on your plate), ½ cup [80 g] of whole olives, two 6 oz [170 g] cans of tuna, and pickled onions (see directions on page 22). Season everything with salt and pepper, then drizzle 3 Tbsp of extra-virgin olive oil over the top and finish with a squeeze of lemon, if you like.

Very Lemony Greens

This recipe is a spin on Greek *horta* and is the answer to the question, "How can I make this meal a little healthier?"

If you're using boxed spinach, partially thaw it before adding it to the pan to help break it up faster.

SERVES 4 TO 6

1 Tbsp kosher salt, plus more for seasoning

Two 10 oz [280 g] bags frozen greens

¼ cup [60 ml] extra-virgin olive oil

Juice of 1 lemon

¼ tsp freshly ground black pepper

In a large pot, bring 6 cups [1.4 L] of water to a boil, then add the salt. Add the greens to the pot and lower the heat so the water simmers steadily. Cook until the greens are silky and tender; for bagged spinach, this could be as little at 5 minutes, and for collards or kale, up to 20 minutes. Drain the greens and shake dry.

Transfer the cooked greens to a large bowl and add the oil, lemon juice, and pepper. Toss gently to dress everything and taste; add more salt, if you like. Serve warm or at room temperature.

MAKE IT A MEAL

Use the greens to make panini by brushing 8 slices of bread on one side with 2 Tbsp of extra-virgin olive oil. Top 4 of the slices with a heaping pile of greens, some crumbled feta cheese (about ⅔ cup [80 g] total), and pickled onions (see directions on page 22). Top with the remaining 4 slices of bread and pan-fry them as you would grilled cheese. Serve hot.

pantry to plate

Beans and Greens

This combination sounds simple but is always more than the sum of its parts. It deserves to be part of your dinner arsenal immediately.

SERVES 3 TO 4

3 Tbsp extra-virgin olive oil

1 garlic clove, peeled and sliced

One 14 oz [400 g] can chickpeas or black beans, drained and rinsed

One 10 oz [280 g] bag frozen greens

1 tsp kosher salt

¼ tsp freshly ground black pepper

Juice of 1 lemon

In a large skillet over medium-high heat, warm the oil with the garlic until the oil shimmers. Add the chickpeas, greens, salt, pepper, and ¼ cup [60 ml] of water and cook, stirring occasionally, until the water has cooked off and the greens are tender, 8 to 10 minutes. Add the lemon juice, stir, and serve hot or at room temperature.

MAKE IT A MEAL
—

Slice or crumble 8 oz [230 g] of Italian sausage into the pan before adding any other ingredients and cook until browned and crisp. Proceed with the recipe and serve with crusty bread.

Garlic Bread

This is a fast fix for when the craving strikes, but I have to admit, it's a pretty good fix.

SERVES 4

4 Tbsp [55 g] butter

1 garlic clove, peeled

½ tsp kosher salt

4 large, or 8 small, slices crusty bread, fully thawed

Preheat the broiler and move the rack as close to the heat source as possible. In a small saucepan over low heat, melt the butter. Use a Microplane to grate the garlic into the butter and cook, swirling the pan often, until the garlic no longer smells raw, 1 to 2 minutes. Add the salt and stir.

Place the bread on a rimmed baking sheet and brush both sides of the slices with the butter mixture. (If you don't have a brush, use a spoon to drizzle the butter over each slice as evenly as possible.) Place the sheet under the broiler and cook—watching very carefully—until the toast is golden around the edges, 3 to 5 minutes. Remove the sheet, carefully flip each slice, and repeat on the other side. Serve hot.

MAKE IT A MEAL

Top with sautéed frozen greens (see page 76 for directions)—or Beans and Greens (page 191)—and one fried egg per person.

pantry to plate

Meals *for* Every Kind of Evening

TRULY 30 MINUTES OR LESS

WEEKEND COOKING

FAMILY FRIENDLY

pantry to plate

Lentil and Sausage Stew 110

Black Bean Tacos 115

Roasted Vegetables with Tahini Sauce 144

Greek Chicken 170

FANCY ENOUGH FOR GUESTS

Crispy Rice Cake with Greens 76

Chicken Paella-ish 78

Not Quite Cacio e Pepe 88

Pasta with Yogurt and Caramelized Onions 92

Kimchi Potato Pancakes 133

Miso Potato Gratin 146

Baked Polenta with Greens and Tomato Sauce 151

Chicken Tagine 164

Coconut-Braised Chicken 168

Lentils in the Style of Cassoulet 177

Sausages Over Polenta 180

VEGAN

VERY PACKABLE,
A.K.A. LUNCH FRIENDLY

Tofu Scramble 25

Spanish Tortilla 41

Crispy Rice Cake with Greens 76

Sesame Noodles 84

Spicy Tuna Pasta 97

Koshari 107

Curried Chickpeas 108

Black Bean Tacos 115

Cabbage Chopped Salad 130

Stewed Potatoes and Broccoli 137

Roasted Vegetables with Tahini Sauce 144

Baked Sweet Potatoes with Spicy Lentils 148

Sausages Over Polenta 180

MAKE AHEAD

ACKNOWLEDGMENTS

◇◇◇◇◇◇◇◇

There are so many people who helped make this the little gem that it is.

Sein Koo, whose illustrations, along with Rachel Harrell's design, turned the recipes into a book I think many people will spend a lot of time with. The warmth and coziness their work brings to mine makes this book so incredibly inviting. I'm in awe of the talent of both of you.

Caroline Schiff, Grace Rosanova, and Jessica Meter, who tested all the recipes and whipped them into shape. This book could not have happened without you.

Alicia Kennedy, Ashley and Danny Ginzberg, James Mayer, Jeanne Brooks, Jerusha Klemperer, Julia Landau, Julia Middleton, Kat Lloyd and Dan Zajackowski, Lydia Berg-Hammond, Mercedes Kraus and Ryan Simons, Nathalie Janson and Michael Eisenbrey, Nona Hurkmans, and Sara Doody, who all took time out of their busy lives to give a recipe or two (or more!) a try.

Angela Miller, who always has my back and great advice.

Claire Gilhuly, for helping me get this project up and running, and answering the occasional panicked email.

Deanne Katz, who has, once again, started with an idea, collaborated every step of the way, and got it to a place I think we're both thrilled with. I too am so glad our paths crossed!

My L&G coworkers, who have also been nothing but supremely supportive and accommodating of my second job.

Annie and Roshan, who tested recipes, provided cute dog pictures, and acted as hype men for my first book. I'm so grateful for all your support.

Mom and Dad, for all your support along the way while I try to make this whole "writing" thing work. You set me up for great success.

And finally, to Amir and Pishi, who, along with a stocked pantry, make our apartment the only place I pretty much ever want to be.

INDEX

◇◇◇◇◇◇◇◇

pantry to plate